VOLU

OLD TESTAMENT

NEW COLLEGEVILLE
BIBLE COMMENTARY

PSALMS 73–150

Dianne Bergant, C.S.A.

SERIES EDITOR

Daniel Durken, O.S.B.

LITURGICAL PRESS
Collegeville, Minnesota

www.litpress.org

Nihil Obstat: Reverend Robert Harren, *Censor deputatus*.
Imprimatur: ✠ Most Reverend John F. Kinney, J.C.D., D.D., Bishop of St. Cloud, Minnesota, August 8, 2013.

Design by Ann Blattner.

Cover illustration: Detail of *Psalms Frontispiece*, Donald Jackson. © 2004 *The Saint John's Bible*, Saint John's University, Collegeville, Minnesota. Used with permission. All rights reserved.

Photos: pages 12, 34, 56, 108, and 114, Thinkstock Photos.

1	2	3	4	5	6	7	8	9

ISBN 978-0-8146-2856-0

CONTENTS

ABBREVIATIONS

Books of the Bible

Acts—Acts of the Apostles
Amos—Amos
Bar—Baruch
1 Chr—1 Chronicles
2 Chr—2 Chronicles
Col—Colossians
1 Cor—1 Corinthians
2 Cor—2 Corinthians
Dan—Daniel
Deut—Deuteronomy
Eccl (or Qoh)—Ecclesiastes
Eph—Ephesians
Esth—Esther
Exod—Exodus
Ezek—Ezekiel
Ezra—Ezra
Gal—Galatians
Gen—Genesis
Hab—Habakkuk
Hag—Haggai
Heb—Hebrews
Hos—Hosea
Isa—Isaiah
Jas—James
Jdt—Judith
Jer—Jeremiah
Job—Job
Joel—Joel
John—John
1 John—1 John
2 John—2 John
3 John—3 John
Jonah—Jonah
Josh—Joshua
Jude—Jude
Judg—Judges
1 Kgs—1 Kings

2 Kgs—2 Kings
Lam—Lamentations
Lev—Leviticus
Luke—Luke
1 Macc—1 Maccabees
2 Macc—2 Maccabees
Mal—Malachi
Mark—Mark
Matt—Matthew
Mic—Micah
Nah—Nahum
Neh—Nehemiah
Num—Numbers
Obad—Obadiah
1 Pet—1 Peter
2 Pet—2 Peter
Phil—Philippians
Phlm—Philemon
Prov—Proverbs
Ps(s)—Psalms
Rev—Revelation
Rom—Romans
Ruth—Ruth
1 Sam—1 Samuel
2 Sam—2 Samuel
Sir—Sirach
Song—Song of Songs
1 Thess—1 Thessalonians
2 Thess—2 Thessalonians
1 Tim—1 Timothy
2 Tim—2 Timothy
Titus—Titus
Tob—Tobit
Wis—Wisdom
Zech—Zechariah
Zeph—Zephaniah

Psalms 73–150

About the book

The book of Psalms, also known as the Psalter, is really a collection of books, each of which ends with a short doxology or hymn of praise: book 1, Psalms 1–41; book 2, Psalms 42–72; book 3, Psalms 73–89; book 4, Psalms 90–106; and book 5, Psalms 107–50. The book of Psalms itself is composed of even earlier collections. Several psalms, found principally in the first book, are attributed to David. (This may account for the popular but probably not historically accurate tradition that David himself wrote most of the psalms.) Several psalms in the second and third books are ascribed to Korah or Asaph, the two great guilds of temple singers of the Second Temple period (cf. 1 Chr 6:33ff; 25:1-2). The fifth book consists of a number of songs of ascent and psalms of praise known as Hallel or the Hallelujah collection. There are also variations in the preferred name for God. *Yahweh* (rendered Lord), generally used in the first, fourth, and fifth collections, suggests an earlier "Yahwist Psalter," while *Elohim* (God) is preferred in the second and third books, suggesting an earlier "Elohist Psalter."

Some psalms include a superscription or an informative statement that precedes the psalm itself. This information might include identification of the earlier collection to which the psalm belonged (e.g., "A psalm of David" [Ps 3] or "A psalm of Asaph" [Ps 82]), liturgical directions (e.g., "For the leader" [Ps 68] or "On stringed instruments" [Ps 55]), lyrical classification (e.g., "A *maskil*" [Ps 54] or "A *miktam*" [Ps 59]), and a purported historical setting (e.g., "For the dedication of the temple" [Ps 30]). This information, which may have little meaning for contemporary readers, was probably included when the psalms were being collected. Since superscriptions are found in the Hebrew text, some English versions begin the numeration of the verses of the psalm with the superscription. The New American Bible Revised Edition follows this custom. Other versions begin the numeration with the first verse of the psalm itself. This explains why there is not always agreement among various translations or versions as to the number of verses in certain psalms.

LITERARY CHARACTERISTICS

The psalms are first and foremost lyrical creations, poems that are rich in metaphor and fashioned according to the patterns and techniques of ancient Israelite poetry. One of the most distinctive characteristics of this type of poetry is its parallelism. In this feature, the second half of a poetic line somehow echoes the sense of the first. Thus we read in Psalm 61:

hear	my cry, O God
listen to	my prayer

This poetic technique serves to intensify the point being made.

Another very important feature found in several psalms is the acrostic structure. In this structure the first letter of the first word of successive poetic lines follows the order of the alphabet. The structure is meant to suggest comprehensiveness, similar to the English expression "from A to Z." Unfortunately, this alphabetic pattern is usually lost when the psalm is translated. However, identification of the acrostic or alphabetic pattern has been retained in Psalms 37, 111, 112, and 119.

A third important feature of the psalms is meter. This is a form of poetic rhythm that is determined by the number of accents in the words that comprise the line of poetry. Since this is a feature of Hebrew poetry, it is also lost in translation.

Finally, a single word, *selah*, is found in several psalms. It is probably an indication of some kind of pause, but it does not always follow the sense of the poem. Many scholars believe that it might have originally functioned as a liturgical or musical directive. However, this is not clear. Nonetheless, it has been retained in the Hebrew and so it does appear in many versions of the Psalter.

Types of psalms

The major classifications of psalms are lament, hymn, prayers of confidence, and prayers of thanksgiving. There are also royal psalms, wisdom poems, historical recitals, ritual or liturgical, and some psalms that might fit more than one classification.

Laments

Nearly a third of all psalms are laments. Some of them are complaints of an individual; others are communal complaints. Laments usually consist of an actual complaint, a plea for deliverance from hardship, an expression of praise of God or confidence that God will intervene and deliver the one(s) suffering, and a promise to perform an act of devotion in gratitude for God's intervention. Some laments include an acknowledgment of guilt or a claim of innocence. Finally, there is frequently a curse hurled at the one(s) believed to be responsible for the intolerable situation that called forth the lament in the first place. Many people believe that originally the lament included several distinct religious sentiments. The first was the lament or complaint. This was followed by expressions of confidence that God would hear the complaint and remedy the situation. The lament would then end with expressions of gratitude for the divine graciousness of which the psalmist was confident. While traces of all three sentiments can still be found in some laments, the confidence and thanksgiving often comprise individual psalms.

Hymns

The hymn consists of a call to praise God and an account of the wondrous acts of God that elicited the praise. These marvelous divine acts might include glories of creation or the marvelous feats performed in history on behalf of Israel. Hymns praising the Lord's kingship are a distinct group of psalms. Their focus is God's cosmic sovereignty and exclusive reign over all the heavenly bodies. Songs of Zion extol God's holy mountain, the place of God's dwelling on earth, and Jerusalem, the city built on that mountain from which God chose to rule.

Prayers of confidence

Although confidence or trust is often found in laments, the Psalter also contains prayers that focus primarily on such sentiments. The motives for confidence in God's protection and care include divine justice that the people believe will be shown on their behalf, God's faithful commitment to the covenant that God chose to initiate with Israel, and the promises made to Israel's ancestors and renewed from generation to generation. As is the case with laments, there are both individual prayers of confidence and those that are communal in character.

Thanksgiving

Scholars do not agree as to which psalms belong to this category because expressions of confidence and gratitude are often found in laments. Consequently, this type of psalm is usually classified according to its content rather than its form. Thanksgiving psalms are similar to hymns, in that they extol the marvelous works of God. However, hymns call forth praise because of these wonders, while thanksgiving psalms include expressions of gratitude for God's graciousness.

7

Royal psalms

Some psalms seem to have sprung from various occasions in the life of the king. They are often referred to as "messianic psalms," since messiah means "anointed one" and kings were anointed. On occasion, they might celebrate the king's success in battle. However, they usually extol the special covenant relationship that God established with the king and the divine protection bestowed on the Israelite rulers because of it. Royal psalms take on new meaning when they are included in the Christian tradition and are applied to Jesus who is king par excellence and the one uniquely anointed by God. In such instances, it is not that the original psalmist had Christ in mind when composing the poem. Rather, the early Christian community began to view Christ from the perspective of the Davidic ruler and to interpret the psalm from a Christian point of view.

Wisdom poems

Wisdom poems clearly differ from other psalms in both content and style. They call people to listen and to learn, not to pray. Although they do not follow a uniform style, they do possess some distinctive literary characteristics. One such characteristic is the acrostic arrangement in which the alphabet determines the initial letter of the first word of each successive line. This is recognizable only in the original Hebrew. A second characteristic is the recourse made to order in the world of nature. This order is employed as an incentive for establishing social order. One of the most prominent topics of the instruction found in these poems is the theory of retribution: the wise or good will be rewarded with happiness and prosperity while the foolish or wicked will suffer misfortune. Descriptions of situations that illustrate this teaching are intended to exhort people to live life in a way that will lead to happiness.

Various other psalms

The songs of ascent, one of the early collections mentioned above, were probably sung during pilgrimages to or processions around Jerusalem and the temple. A few other psalms appear to have been composed in the style of prophetic speech. Finally, a small number of psalms defy classification. They are either historical recountings of the feats of the Lord, composites of other psalm forms, celebrations of the kingship of the Lord, or liturgical songs.

THE THEOLOGY IN THE PSALMS

The God of Israel

The portrait of God sketched in the psalms draws together all the characterizations of God found in the rest of the Israelite tradition. God is depicted as the creator of the universe and the source of all life, victoriously enthroned in heaven, yet dwelling in the city of Jerusalem. Initially believed to be exclusively Israel's liberator, God's reign was ultimately perceived as universal, and all people were invited to worship this God in Jerusalem. The God depicted in the psalms inspires both fear and confidence because of God's breathtaking divine power and majesty as well as the care and protection that God provided for Israel's ancestors in the past. This God demands compliance to the law and yet forgives infraction of it, regardless of the seriousness of the violation. Perhaps the key characterization of the Lord is that of "covenant partner." Fundamental to this understanding of God is the firm conviction that God initiated the covenant, not because Israel in any way deserved it, but because God is "gracious and merciful, slow to anger and abounding in love" (Pss 145:8; 103:8).

Humankind

The psalms come from a society in which men are the norm and so the language and imagery reflect this gender bias. Honored as the culmination of creation, humankind is made responsible for all other living creatures. Still, humans live a fleeting life, perishing after a short life span like field flowers. The absence of a clear notion of life after death underscores the starkness of life's impermanence. Though all humans are dependent on God's providence, God seems to be the special guardian of the poor and afflicted, the defenseless widows and orphans.

Natural creation

The psalms reveal a special regard for creation as the handiwork of God's power and ingenuity. Furthermore, Israel reinterpreted many ancient Near Eastern concepts of divinity, arguing that its own God is the one revealed through the elements of nature, in the exquisite design of the natural world, in the power of the thunderstorm, and in the gentleness of refreshing rain. In many psalms creation itself is called on to join in the praise of this wondrous creator-God.

The future

Israel's view of the future, known as eschatology, stems from its faith in the goodness of God toward all creation. Despite the struggles that it faced throughout its history, Israel believed that the final victory would be God's. The psalms say very little about possible life beyond the grave, but they frequently mention the shadowy existence known as Sheol. This netherworld was not a place of reward or punishment, but of darkness, dust, and inactivity. Israel may not have had a clear idea of life after death, but it did not seem to believe that the dead ceased to exist. The people awaited a final divine victory that would unfold in history, but in a history that included the cosmic realm of the heavens as well.

THE PSALMS TODAY

Contemporary devotion

The psalms continue to play a significant role in the official and private prayer of both the Jewish and Christian communities today. In this way they shape the minds and hearts of modern believers. One result of the various liturgical reforms of the twentieth century is that verses from a particular psalm serve as a response to the first reading. When there is a thematic connection between that first reading and the gospel passage, the responsorial psalm often acts as a prayerful summation of the readings.

Reflective reading of the psalms enables us to immerse ourselves in the religious dispositions of the psalmist. Though the sentiments with which we come to the psalms may not be identical to those expressed in those prayers, we can still recognize the world that they project. At the moment, we may not be living in a world similar to what is depicted there, and our sentiments may not correspond to the sentiments expressed by the psalmist. Most likely, however, there are people somewhere for whom those sentiments accurately express their present situation. Standing in solidarity with those people, we can make our prayer their prayer. In this way our religious consciousness can be profoundly shaped by the psalms.

Troublesome images

The psalms come from worlds that are very different from those of contemporary society. They frequently reflect cultural customs and values that are foreign to us or might even offend our sensitivities. Examples of the first would be ancient patriarchal marriage practices or family customs; an example of the second would be the role that honor and shame plays in determining one's social status. In such situations it is important to discover the meaning behind the uncommon expression or figure of speech in order to appreciate its theological message. This can usually be accomplished through an examination of the historical circumstances from which the psalm originated.

There are other aspects of the psalms that many people today find offensive. Examples of these would include the male bias that is apparent in the gender-specific language used, the ethnocentrism that reveals itself in a measure of disdain for nations other than Israel, and the prejudice in presuming that physical disabilities are punishment for sin. These offensive features are not easily overlooked, but careful historical analysis can help us realize that they are historically and culturally conditioned perspectives that need not be carried into a contemporary point of view.

What is perhaps most troublesome today in many circles is the violence that seems to enjoy divine sanction in so many of the psalms. The psalmists perceive God as a warrior who can be called on to wreak vengeance on the heads of Israel's opponents. God is called on to "crush the heads of his enemies" and then directs the people to "wash your feet in your enemy's blood" (Ps 68:22, 24). Who can comfortably pray: "Blessed the one who seizes your children / and smashes them against the rock" (Ps 137:9)? This kind of characterization of God and these kinds of directives must be carefully interpreted if we are to continue to maintain that they have revelatory value for us today.

Without in any way minimizing what is offensive, we should realize that the psalmists understand the violence that they attributed to God as a form of divine retribution. God was being called on to punish the wicked. When these wicked people were the national enemies of Israel, God was envisioned as a defending warrior, fighting on Israel's side. Since the image of a conquering god was already present in the ancient myths of creation, it is not difficult to see how such an understanding of God might be employed to describe how God acted in Israel's military history.

As is the case with all characterizations of God, the image of the divine warrior is a metaphor, a figure of speech that applies traits of one object to a second and very different object. A metaphor is never a definition, nor does it exactly parallel the two objects being compared. It simply states how these two objects have certain attributes in common. If we are to understand the metaphor of God the warrior, we will have to discover what traits traditionally attributed to the warrior are being applied to God.

Psalms 73–150

Third Book—Psalms 73–89

The Trial of the Just

73 ¹A psalm of Asaph.

How good God is to the upright,
to those who are pure of heart!

I

²But, as for me, my feet had almost
stumbled;
my steps had nearly slipped,

³Because I was envious of the
arrogant
when I saw the prosperity of the
wicked.
⁴For they suffer no pain;
their bodies are healthy and
sleek.
⁵They are free of the burdens of life;
they are not afflicted like others.
⁶Thus pride adorns them as a
necklace;
violence clothes them as a robe.

BOOK THREE: PSALMS 73–89

This third book of psalms contains the major collection of psalms from the collection associated with Asaph.

Psalm 73 (wisdom psalm)

The psalm is difficult to classify. However, since its chief focus is the theme of retribution, many commentators consider it a wisdom psalm.

1b God rewards the righteous

The psalm opens stating the first half of the theory of retribution: the good will be rewarded. It is a curious opening statement for a psalm that really describes the dilemma suffered by the psalmist at the sight of the prosperity of the wicked.

2-5 The wicked enjoy life

The psalmist is troubled by the prosperity (the Hebrew is *shalom*) of the wicked. These wicked people should be suffering the consequences of their sinful way of living. Instead, they seem to be thriving. It is not their ungodly behavior that is coveted by the psalmist, but the apparent ease of their lives.

13

"Terrible and awesome are you, stronger than the ancient mountains" (Ps 76:5).

⁷Out of such blindness comes sin;
    evil thoughts flood their hearts.
⁸They scoff and spout their malice;
    from on high they utter threats.
⁹They set their mouths against the
      heavens,
    their tongues roam the earth.
¹⁰So my people turn to them
    and drink deeply of their words.
¹¹They say, "Does God really
      know?"
    "Does the Most High have any
      knowledge?"
¹²Such, then, are the wicked,

always carefree, increasing their
    wealth.

II

¹³Is it in vain that I have kept my
    heart pure,
    washed my hands in innocence?
¹⁴For I am afflicted day after day,
    chastised every morning.
¹⁵Had I thought, "I will speak as
    they do,"
I would have betrayed this
    generation of your
    children.

They are healthy and free of life's cares. They do not carry the burdens that many of the innocent do. Not only do the wicked seem to prosper, but it appears that those who should be enjoying life's blessings are not. In other words, the entire theory of retribution is reversed: those who should not be happy enjoy life; those who should be happy suffer. It is this incongruity that so troubles the psalmist.

6-12 The arrogance of the wicked

The wicked themselves realize that the circumstances of their lives do not fit the pattern established by the theory of retribution. However, unlike the psalmist, they are not bothered by this. Rather, they delight in it. They wrap themselves in their sinfulness as they would clothe themselves in garments. Their good fortune makes them haughty. They scorn whatever in heaven or on earth might challenge them. They even defy God, maintaining that God really does not know what is happening in the world. Such blasphemy challenges one of God's fundamental attributes, namely, divine omniscience. To say that God does not know implies that God will be unable to rectify the situation. This is an indirect challenge to divine omnipotence. The circumstances of the wicked are succinctly summarized: they are free of cares, and they amass wealth.

13-17 The heart of the psalmist

In the face of the prosperity of the wicked, the psalmist questions the value of loyal commitment to God. If the force of retribution has been turned upside down, why struggle to be faithful? A clean or pure heart and hands washed in innocence not only refer to personal moral integrity, but also are the criteria for access to the temple and the presence of God (cf. Ps 24:3-6).

¹⁶Though I tried to understand all
this,
it was too difficult for me,
¹⁷Till I entered the sanctuary of God
and came to understand their
end.

III

¹⁸You set them, indeed, on a
slippery road;
you hurl them down to ruin.
¹⁹How suddenly they are devastated;
utterly undone by disaster!
²⁰They are like a dream after
waking, Lord,
dismissed like shadows when
you arise.

IV

²¹Since my heart was embittered
and my soul deeply wounded,
²²I was stupid and could not
understand;
I was like a brute beast in your
presence.
²³Yet I am always with you;
you take hold of my right hand.
²⁴With your counsel you guide me,
and at the end receive me with
honor.
²⁵Whom else have I in the heavens?
None beside you delights me on
earth.
²⁶Though my flesh and my heart
fail,

The psalmist has lived with this kind of integrity, yet has endured constant affliction. Despite this, any decision to join the ranks of the wicked is firmly rejected, because it would be a sign of betrayal of God's people. Still, like Job, the psalmist struggles to understand the incongruity of these circumstances.

Verse 17 announces a turning point in the psalmist's struggle. From a literary point of view, it also acts as a kind of hinge, connecting this struggle with insight into the ultimate end of the wicked, which is described in the verses that follow. This shift in understanding took place in the sanctuary. Hence the psalmist claims to possess the kind of integrity required for entrance into God's holy place.

18-20 The fate of the wicked

The ultimate fate of the wicked is described in graphic terms. God caused them to slip and fall from prominence into ruin. This fall was not gradual. It was total, unforeseen, and compounded by all of the surprise and terror that accompanies sudden disaster. The period of the wicked's prosperity is characterized as a time when God was asleep, unaware of the inequity of the situation. But now that the Lord is awake and the ungodly have been dealt the just desserts of their sinfulness, they are like a bad dream. They have no lasting force.

21-28 Confidence is restored

Personal affliction that is incomprehensible along with the apparent good fortune of the wicked left the psalmist deeply wounded and embittered and

God is the rock of my heart, my
portion forever.
27But those who are far from you
perish;
you destroy those unfaithful to
you.
28As for me, to be near God is my
good,
to make the Lord GOD my refuge.
I shall declare all your works
in the gates of daughter Zion.

**Prayer at the Destruction of the
Temple**

74 1A *maskil* of Asaph.

I

Why, God, have you cast us off
forever?

Why does your anger burn
against the sheep of your
pasture?
2Remember your people, whom
you acquired of old,
the tribe you redeemed as your
own heritage,
Mount Zion where you dwell.
3Direct your steps toward the utter
destruction,
everything the enemy laid waste
in the sanctuary.
4Your foes roared triumphantly in
the place of your assembly;
they set up their own tokens of
victory.
5They hacked away like a forester
gathering boughs,
swinging his ax in a thicket of
trees.

acting like a senseless brute animal. The psalmist should have known that
God would eventually intervene and correct the situation. Once confidence
in divine fairness is restored, the psalmist professes enduring attachment
to God alone and commitment to God's guidance. God is the rock on which
the psalmist finds security, the portion to which the psalmist can lay claim.
Though the wicked will perish, the psalmist will remain near to God and
will announce God's goodness to all who will hear.

Psalm 74 (communal lament)

1-3 The lament and the prayer

The people feel that they have been cast off and forgotten by God. In
their name, the psalmist cries in lament: "Why?" What have they done to
deserve this? They are God's flock, God's own people, the tribe that God
brought back. Mount Zion with its sacred temple is the place where God
chose to dwell. Why has God turned against them? The plea is twofold:
remember this people; return to the ravaged sanctuary. "Remember" means
"turn back and remedy the situation." The psalmist is certain that walking
through the ruins of the temple will cause God to relent.

4-9 The destruction of the sanctuary

The enemies of God ravaged the holy place, slashing away at the wood
of the shrine as if it were an overgrown grove of trees, destroying what they

⁶They smashed all its engraved
work,
struck it with ax and pick.
⁷They set your sanctuary on fire,
profaned your name's abode by
razing it to the ground.
⁸They said in their hearts, "We will
destroy them all!
Burn all the assembly-places of
God in the land!"
⁹Even so we have seen no signs for
us,
there is no prophet any more,
no one among us who knows
for how long.
¹⁰How long, O God, will the enemy
jeer?
Will the enemy revile your name
forever?
¹¹Why draw back your hand,
why hold back your right hand
within your bosom?

II

¹²Yet you, God, are my king from of
old,
winning victories throughout
the earth.
¹³You stirred up the sea by your
might;
you smashed the heads of the
dragons on the waters.
¹⁴You crushed the heads of
Leviathan,
gave him as food to the sharks.
¹⁵You opened up springs and
torrents,
brought dry land out of the
primeval waters.

could, and finally setting it on fire. As a result, the devout praise of God has given way to the enemies' mocking shouts of victory; the sacred furnishings have been replaced by their victorious standards of war. God's holy place has been both desecrated and destroyed. The evil foes have even issued the command to lay waste all the other shrines in the land. This detailed description has led many commentators to date the psalm at the time of the exile or shortly after it.

In the past, the people looked for signs that might have helped them discover God's will. Prophets also had arisen through whom God would speak to the people. Now they have neither signs nor prophets, so they have no way of knowing how long this devastation might last.

10-11 A second lament

Again the psalmist cries out: "How long?" This time the concern is with the way the enemy blasphemes God. How long will God allow this to last? Why does God not retaliate? The right hand represents the hand with which one fights, the hand that holds the weapon. It seems that God's right hand is idle.

12-17 The creative power of God

It is not that God is powerless. On the contrary, this God has not only been victorious throughout the earth, but in the beginning actually

¹⁶Yours the day and yours the night
  too;
  you set the moon and sun in
    place.
¹⁷You fixed all the limits of the earth;
  summer and winter you made.
¹⁸Remember how the enemy has
    jeered, LORD,
  how a foolish people has reviled
    your name.
¹⁹Do not surrender to wild animals
    those who praise you;
  do not forget forever the life of
    your afflicted.

²⁰Look to your covenant,
  for the recesses of the land
  are full of the haunts of violence.
²¹Let not the oppressed turn back in
    shame;
  may the poor and needy praise
    your name.
²²Arise, God, defend your cause;
  remember the constant jeering
    of the fools.
²³Do not forget the clamor of your
    foes,
  the unceasing uproar of your
    enemies.

conquered the forces of creation as well. In the myths of creation, the sea was the god of chaos. Another fearsome threat was the dragon or mighty creature of the deep called Leviathan (cf. Isa 27:1; Job 3:8; 40:25). The psalmist declares that God exercised power over all these mythological beings as well. Creation, often characterized as victory over chaos, is here described as the simple ordering of nature. God's control of water embraces the management of springs and torrents on earth as well. Through governance of the heavenly bodies, God regulates days and nights and the seasons of the year.

18-23 A plea for divine justice

Once again the psalmist prays that God might remember. This time it is a prayer to remember justice, specifically punishment of the wicked who taunted God. Since part of one's very person was somehow contained in one's name, to profane God's name was to blaspheme God. This is what the enemy has done. On the other hand, just as the psalmist would have God recall the sinner, so would the psalmist have God be attentive to the needs of the righteous. "[W]ild animals" could be read literally or it might be a figurative way of referring to the enemies. The psalmist prays: Don't surrender your people to the beasts; don't forget their lives; look to the covenant and the promise of protection that it contains. The psalmist would have God look kindly on God's own people but punish severely those who stand against them and against God.

God the Judge of the World

75 ¹For the leader. Do not destroy!
A psalm of Asaph; a song.

I

²We thank you, God, we give thanks;
we call upon your name,
we declare your wonderful
deeds.
[You said:]
³"I will choose the time;
I will judge fairly.
⁴Though the earth and all its
inhabitants quake,
I make steady its pillars."

Selah

II

⁵So I say to the boastful: "Do not
boast!"
to the wicked: "Do not raise
your horns!
⁶Do not raise your horns against
heaven!
Do not speak with a stiff neck!"
⁷For judgment comes not from east
or from west,
not from the wilderness or the
mountains,
⁸But from God who decides,
who brings some low and raises
others high.
⁹Yes, a cup is in the LORD's hand,
foaming wine, fully spiced.

Psalm 75 (prophetic exhortation)

2 Praise of God

The psalm opens with words of praise and thanksgiving. (The phrase "call upon your name" might be better translated "your name is near," suggesting that God is already close to the psalmist.) Though the works of creation are often called wondrous deeds, here the reference is probably to divine judgment.

3-6 God speaks

God claims to exercise universal and exclusive control: "I will choose . . . / I will judge . . . / I make steady." The time of judgment is probably a reference to divine intervention in the future, a time that only God knows. Though the judgment will be demanding, it will be fair. Though earth and everything on it will quake, God will not allow it to collapse. God warns the boastful and the wicked that they will be powerless when this comes to pass. The horn is a symbol of strength. When God comes to judge the earth, human strength will be useless.

7-9 God's judgment

The psalmist expands God's words about divine judgment. At different times in its history, Israel experienced attacks from enemy nations in the east and from some in the west. This included marauders from the wilderness. This does not constitute the judgment of which God or the psalmist speaks. The judgment referred to here comes from God, who lifts some up

19

When God pours it out,
   they will drain it even to the
      dregs;
   all the wicked of the earth will
      drink.
¹⁰But I will rejoice forever;
   I will sing praise to the God of
      Jacob,
¹¹[Who has said:]
"I will cut off all the horns of the
      wicked,
   but the horns of the righteous
      will be exalted."

God Defends Zion

76 ¹For the leader; a psalm with stringed instruments. A song of Asaph.

I

²Renowned in Judah is God,
   whose name is great in Israel.
³On Salem is God's tent, his shelter
      on Zion.
⁴There the flashing arrows were
      shattered,
   shield, sword, and weapons of
      war.

                              Selah

II

⁵Terrible and awesome are you,
   stronger than the ancient
      mountains.
⁶Despoiled are the stouthearted;
   they sank into sleep;

and puts others down. The cup mentioned is the cup of divine wrath (cf. Isa 51:17; Jer 25:15; Ezek 23:33). The guilty will be forced to drink of it.

10-11 Final praise of God

The psalm ends as it began, with praise of God. The title "God of Jacob" identifies God as the special divine patron of Israel. This suggests that the wicked are not merely sinners, but are the enemies of Israel. The reference gives a national character to this psalm.

Psalm 76 (song of Zion)

2-4 Praise of Zion

Judah is the name of the southern kingdom within which Jerusalem and the temple were located. It was God's choice of this place that gave the region its importance. Since God's name is an aspect of God's very being, the divine name itself is renowned. Salem may have been the original name of the city (cf. Gen 14:18). It is there, in the temple in that city on that mountain, that God decided to dwell. Though the city was won through war (cf. 2 Sam 5:6-12), God's presence makes the city secure and weapons of war are now unnecessary.

5-11 God's defense

God is described as a mighty and fearsome warrior, one before whom all else tremble. The ancient mountains could be a reference to the foundations of the universe. Since God established them, God's strength would

the hands of all the men of valor
have failed.
⁷At your roar, O God of Jacob,
chariot and steed lay still.
⁸You, terrible are you;
who can stand before you and
your great anger?
⁹From the heavens you pronounced
sentence;
the earth was terrified and
reduced to silence,
¹⁰When you arose, O God, for
judgment
to save the afflicted of the land.

Selah

¹¹Surely the wrath of man will give
you thanks;

the remnant of your furor will
keep your feast.

III

¹²Make and keep vows to the LORD
your God.
May all around him bring gifts
to the one to be feared,
¹³Who checks the spirit of princes,
who is fearful to the kings of
earth.

Confidence in God During National Distress

77 ¹For the leader; According to
Jeduthun. A psalm of Asaph.

certainly exceed theirs. Chariots and steeds call to mind God's triumph over the Egyptians at the time of the Exodus (cf. Exod 14:26-31). Divine anger is not capricious. It is righteous anger in the face of willful transgression. The punishment that God metes out is equitable judgment. God's roar could be the judgment that God pronounces from heaven.

Edom was one of the nations east of the Jordan River. It had a long and varied history with Israel. It was somehow linked with Israel through Jacob's twin brother Esau (cf. Gen 25:22-26), yet it was also considered an enemy because it refused passageway when Israel moved into Canaan (cf. Num 20:18). Hamath was part of the land in the north occupied by Israel (cf. Num 34:7-9). In this psalm, however, both nations pay homage to the God of Israel.

12-13 The people's response

The psalmist calls on the people to fulfill their religious obligations. They are to bring offerings to the temple. For the third time God is called awesome (vv. 5, 8, 12). In the previous instances the focus was on God's military prowess. Here it describes the status that God enjoys among the rulers of the earth.

Psalm 77 (lament of an individual)

2-4 Lament

The cry of lament is searing and prolonged. It rings out to God day and night, and the psalmist refuses to be consoled by anything or anyone other

I

²I cry aloud to God,
  I cry to God to hear me.
³On the day of my distress I seek
    the Lord;
  by night my hands are stretched
    out unceasingly;
  I refuse to be consoled.
⁴When I think of God, I groan;
  as I meditate, my spirit grows
    faint.

Selah

⁵You have kept me from closing my
    eyes in sleep;
  I am troubled and cannot speak.
⁶I consider the days of old;
  the years long past ⁷I remember.
At night I ponder in my heart;
  and as I meditate, my spirit
    probes:

⁸"Will the Lord reject us forever,
  never again show favor?
⁹Has God's mercy ceased forever?
  The promise to go unfulfilled
    for future ages?
¹⁰Has God forgotten how to show
    mercy,
  in anger withheld his
    compassion?"

Selah

¹¹I conclude: "My sorrow is this,
  the right hand of the Most High
    has abandoned us."

II

¹²I will recall the deeds of the LORD;
  yes, recall your wonders of old.
¹³I will ponder all your works;
  on your exploits I will meditate.
¹⁴Your way, God, is holy;
  what god is as great as our God?

---

than God. However, it is actually the thought of God that causes the psalmist to lament. (Throughout the psalm, the perspective moves from the individual to the community.)

5-11 The psalmist's suffering

The psalmist suffers great mental anguish. This includes inner turmoil, sleeplessness, and the inability to communicate. Usually remembrance of "the days of old," a reference to the former time of deliverance, brings confidence in God. Such is not the case here. Instead, memory of past deliverance only exaggerates the present tribulation. God may have intervened in the past, but there is no indication that God will do so in the present. This only causes more anxiety. In fact, the psalmist wonders if perhaps God has terminated the covenantal relationship. Where are the covenant love, mercy, and compassion? Have God's promises been negated? The right hand of God is the hand that protects. It should have been raised in Israel's defense. The psalmist's suffering raises the question: has God's protection been withdrawn?

12-16 Past deliverance

These afflictions notwithstanding, the psalmist is intent on not only remembering the past gracious deeds of the Lord but also proclaiming them

¹⁵You are the God who does
    wonders;
    among the peoples you have
        revealed your might.
¹⁶With your mighty arm you
    redeemed your people,
    the children of Jacob and Joseph.

                Selah

¹⁷The waters saw you, God;
    the waters saw you and lashed
    about,
    even the deeps of the sea
    trembled.
¹⁸The clouds poured down their
    rains;

the thunderheads rumbled;
    your arrows flashed back and
    forth.
¹⁹The thunder of your chariot
    wheels resounded;
    your lightning lit up the world;
    the earth trembled and quaked.
²⁰Through the sea was your way;
    your path, through the mighty
    waters,
    though your footsteps were
    unseen.
²¹You led your people like a flock
    by the hand of Moses and
    Aaron.

---

to others. The reference here is probably to the deliverance of the people of Israel. God could wield saving power in the land of another people, within the jurisdiction of another god. God did this at the time of the deliverance out of Egypt. Why not now? God was able to do this because there is no god greater than the God of Israel. Though the psalm speaks of Jacob and Joseph, names often given to the northern tribes, the psalmist probably has the entire nation in mind.

17-21 God's cosmic power

The warrior God who saved Israel is also the creator God who in the beginning brought order to the entire cosmos. Just as God conquered Israel's national enemies, so God subdued the cosmic forces. The waters of chaos were no match for the mighty God. They are now tamed and, by the power of God, have become mere natural phenomena. God is characterized as the storm deity who races across the heavens. It is this God who controls the rains, whose arrows are seen in the lightning, and whose chariot wheels can be heard in the thunder.

The image of a divine warrior traveling in a chariot remains the same, but the setting changes. The psalm moves from a cosmic setting in the heavens to a historical setting on earth. The waters, once a cosmic threat, are now the sea through which God's people pass. There is little difference between control of the waters of chaos and those of the Reed Sea, for the cosmic creator and the God who saved Israel through the leadership of Moses and Aaron are one and the same God.

A New Beginning in Zion and David

78 [1]A *maskil* of Asaph.

I

Attend, my people, to my teaching;
 listen to the words of my mouth.
[2]I will open my mouth in a parable,
 unfold the puzzling events of
 the past.
[3]What we have heard and know;
 things our ancestors have
 recounted to us.
[4]We do not keep them from our
 children;
 we recount them to the next
 generation,
The praiseworthy deeds of the
 LORD and his strength,
 the wonders that he performed.
[5]God made a decree in Jacob,
 established a law in Israel:
Which he commanded our
 ancestors,

they were to teach their
 children;
[6]That the next generation might
 come to know,
 children yet to be born.
In turn they were to recount them
 to their children,
[7]that they too might put their
 confidence in God,
And not forget God's deeds,
 but keep his commandments.
[8]They were not to be like their
 ancestors,
 a rebellious and defiant
 generation,
A generation whose heart was not
 constant,
 and whose spirit was not faithful
 to God.
[9]The ranks of Ephraimite archers,
 retreated on the day of battle.
[10]They did not keep God's covenant;
 they refused to walk according
 to his law.

Psalm 78 (historical recital)

1-11 Introduction

This historical recital is an unusual kind of psalm. While it recounts the marvelous deeds of God, it does so for the purpose of teaching others rather than praising God. Furthermore, the purpose of the teaching is clearly stated. Lessons are to be drawn from the past. Those who hear the report are to put their trust in God and not, like the ancestors who actually experienced the wondrous deed, rebel against God (cf. Deut 9:7, 24). In other words, the purpose of the retelling is obedience to the law (*torah*, v. 5).

The psalm opens like a wisdom psalm: "Attend . . . listen." The psalmist is about to explain a story. The Hebrew *mashal* might be better translated as the generic word "proverb," a lesson from life. The traditional accounts are well known: our ancestors knew them; we know them; and our children—even those yet to be born—will know them. The stories may be known, but the lessons to be drawn from them are more difficult to discern. An example was given from the dismal history of the northern kingdom. (Ephraim, the name of one tribe, also referred to all of the tribes of the north.) It is the psalmist's way of saying: let this be a lesson to you.

[11]They forgot his deeds,
the wonders that he had shown
them.

II

A

[12]In the sight of their ancestors God
did wonders,
in the land of Egypt, the plain of
Zoan.
[13]He split the sea and led them
across,
making the waters stand like
walls.
[14]He led them with a cloud by day,
all night with the light of fire.
[15]He split rocks in the desert,
gave water to drink, abundant
as the deeps of the sea.
[16]He made streams flow from crags,
caused rivers of water to flow
down.

B

[17]But they went on sinning against
him,
rebelling against the Most High
in the desert.
[18]They tested God in their hearts,
demanding the food they craved.
[19]They spoke against God, and said,
"Can God spread a table in the
wilderness?
[20]True, when he struck the rock,
water gushed forth,
the wadies flooded.
But can he also give bread,
or provide meat to his people?"

C

[21]The LORD heard and grew angry;
fire blazed up against Jacob;
anger flared up against Israel.
[22]For they did not believe in God,
did not trust in his saving
power.

12-16 Egypt and the wilderness

The mighty power of God was seen in the marvels performed in the land of Egypt, where God split the sea just as the primordial waters of chaos had been defeated at the time of creation. The wondrous deeds did not end there. Just as God led the people through the waters, so God led them through the wilderness by day and by night and supplied them with water from the rock. God was not only their savior but also their provider.

17-20 The people sinned

The rebellion of the people is inexplicable. Deliverance did not seem to have been enough for them, nor was the miracle of water from the rock. They demanded food. This was not the first time that they had rebelled. The psalm says that they "went on sinning." In fact, they put God to the test, a sign that they lacked trust in God's power or in God's willingness to care for them.

21-32 God's response

God's initial response to their lack of trust was rage. What follows is curious. Rather than strike them down, God gave them what they

²³So he commanded the clouds
above;
and opened the doors of heaven.
²⁴God rained manna upon them for
food;
grain from heaven he gave
them.
²⁵Man ate the bread of the angels;
food he sent in abundance.
²⁶He stirred up the east wind in the
skies;
by his might God brought on
the south wind.
²⁷He rained meat upon them like
dust,
winged fowl like the sands of
the sea,
²⁸They fell down in the midst of
their camp,
all round their dwellings.
²⁹They ate and were well filled;
he gave them what they had
craved.
³⁰But while they still wanted more,
and the food was still in their
mouths,
³¹God's anger flared up against
them,
and he made a slaughter of their
strongest,
laying low the youth of Israel.

³²In spite of all this they went on
sinning,
they did not believe in his
wonders.

D

³³God ended their days abruptly,
their years in sudden death.
³⁴When he slew them, they began to
seek him;
they again looked for God.
³⁵They remembered that God was
their rock,
God Most High, their redeemer.
³⁶But they deceived him with their
mouths,
lied to him with their tongues.
³⁷Their hearts were not constant
toward him;
they were not faithful to his
covenant.
³⁸But God being compassionate forgave their sin;
he did not utterly destroy them.
Time and again he turned back his
anger,
unwilling to unleash all his rage.
³⁹He remembered that they were
flesh,
a breath that passes on and does
not return.

---

demanded. The heavens opened and manna rained down; God stirred up the east wind and it brought winged fowl. The people ate and were more than satisfied. However, God's anger had not been abated. While they were still eating, it flared up and consumed the strongest among them, the promise of their future. As unbelievable as it may seem, the people continued in their rebellion and lack of faith.

33-39 The covenant relationship

When Israel recounts its history, it always underscores God's continued care despite the people's fickleness. God may be wrathful, but divine anger was always precipitated by infidelity. For a time the people might have remembered God's constancy toward them, but then they fell back into their old ways of sin. They were not faithful to the covenant, but God con-

III

A

⁴⁰How often they rebelled against
God in the wilderness,
grieved him in the wasteland.
⁴¹Again and again they tested God,
provoked the Holy One of
Israel.
⁴²They did not remember his power,
the day he redeemed them from
the foe,
⁴³When he performed his signs in
Egypt,
his wonders in the plain of
Zoan.
⁴⁴God turned their rivers to blood;
their streams they could not
drink.
⁴⁵He sent swarms of insects that
devoured them,
frogs that destroyed them.
⁴⁶He gave their harvest to the
caterpillar,
the fruits of their labor to the
locust.
⁴⁷He killed their vines with hail,
their sycamores with frost.
⁴⁸He exposed their cattle to plague,
their flocks to pestilence.

⁴⁹He let loose against them the heat
of his anger,
wrath, fury, and distress,
a band of deadly messengers.
⁵⁰He cleared a path for his anger;
he did not spare them from
death,
but delivered their animals to
the plague.
⁵¹He struck all the firstborn of
Egypt,
the first fruits of their vigor in
the tents of Ham.
⁵²Then God led forth his people like
sheep,
guided them like a flock
through the wilderness.
⁵³He led them on secure and
unafraid,
while the sea enveloped their
enemies.
⁵⁴And he brought them to his holy
mountain,
the hill his right hand had won.
⁵⁵He drove out the nations before
them,
allotted them as their inherited
portion,
and settled in their tents the
tribes of Israel.

tinued to be merciful toward them. The frailty of human nature is given as
a reason for God's forgiveness.

40-55 Deliverance and entrance into the land

The remainder of the psalm repeats and enlarges many of the themes
recounted in the preceding verses, almost as if these were two psalms joined
together. The psalmist recalls the rebellion of Israel (cf. vv. 12-16) and adds
an account of the plagues that struck Egypt but spared God's people (cf.
Exod 7–11). All these marvels originated from the hand of God, and yet the
people rebelled and tested God. Finally, God brought them to a holy land
and allotted the territory to the various tribes. These were the events that
established Israel as a nation chosen by God from among all other nations.
Surely their gratitude would be shown in their obedience.

B

56But they tested and rebelled
    against God Most High,
  his decrees they did not observe.
57They turned disloyal, faithless like
    their ancestors;
  they proved false like a slack
    bow.
58They enraged him with their high
    places,
  and with their idols provoked
    him to jealous anger.

his glorious ark into the hands
    of the foe.
62God delivered his people to the
    sword;
  he was enraged against his
    heritage.
63Fire consumed their young men;
  their young women heard no
    wedding songs.
64Their priests fell by the sword;
  their widows made no
    lamentation.

C

59God heard and grew angry;
  he rejected Israel completely.
60He forsook the shrine at Shiloh,
  the tent he set up among human
    beings.
61He gave up his might into
    captivity,

D

65Then the Lord awoke as from
    sleep,
  like a warrior shouting from the
    effects of wine.
66He put his foes to flight;
  everlasting shame he dealt
    them.

56-58 A second rebellious generation

The first part of this report of the sinfulness of the people resembles an earlier summary (cf. vv. 17-20). However, just as the previous verses added mention of the occupation of the land, so these verses tell of the idolatry of the people at that time in their history. That generation succumbed to the worship of Canaanite gods, worship that was performed at various high places in the area. These people were no better than their ancestors.

59-64 God's response

Once again, God's anger blazed against the sinfulness of the people. As before (cf. vv. 21-32), this anger was a response to their disregard for the covenant responsibilities to which they had agreed. As punishment for their transgressions in the land, God withheld divine protection and allowed victory to their enemies. The ark of the covenant, the symbol of God's presence in their midst, was captured and taken from the tribal shrine at Shiloh. Their warriors were killed and the rest of the nation suffered severely.

65-72 The choice of David

God's anger does not last forever. The earlier verses told of God's covenantal faithfulness and mercy (cf. vv. 33-39). This final section tells of another special relationship, the one God made with David. Here God's

⁶⁷He rejected the tent of Joseph,
　　chose not the tribe of Ephraim.
⁶⁸God chose the tribe of Judah,
　　Mount Zion which he loved.
⁶⁹He built his shrine like the heavens,
　　like the earth which he founded
　　　forever.
⁷⁰He chose David his servant,
　　took him from the sheepfolds.
⁷¹From tending ewes God brought
　　him,
　　to shepherd Jacob, his people,
　　Israel, his heritage.
⁷²He shepherded them with a pure
　　heart;
　　with skilled hands he guided
　　　them.

A Prayer for Jerusalem

79 ¹A psalm of Asaph.

I

O God, the nations have invaded
　　your inheritance;
　　they have defiled your holy
　　　temple;
　　they have laid Jerusalem in
　　　ruins.
²They have left the corpses of your
　　servants
　　as food for the birds of the sky,
　　the flesh of those devoted to you
　　　for the beasts of the earth.
³They have poured out their blood
　　like water
　　all around Jerusalem,
　　and no one is left to do the
　　　burying.
⁴We have become the reproach of
　　our neighbors,
　　the scorn and derision of those
　　　around us.

---

preference for the southern kingdom is obvious. God is said to have rejected the northern tribes of Joseph and Ephraim in favor of choosing a king from the southern tribe of Judah. Furthermore, Mount Zion, on which was built Jerusalem, the city of David, was the place God chose to dwell. David, the former shepherd, was appointed the shepherd of God's own people, the people who, generation after generation, sinned against God. Despite their weaknesses, this king was both a skillful ruler and a righteous man.

The psalm ends on this positive note. The extent of the people's sinfulness could never compare with the depth of God's love. As stated at the beginning, those hearing the story are encouraged to refrain from following the example of their ancestors, but rather to be faithful to the covenant made with God (vv. 6-8).

Psalm 79 (communal lament)

1-4 The cruelty of the enemies

The psalm has traditionally been linked with the destruction of Jerusalem and the desecration of the temple. The description of the horrors that befell the people is startling. Death and devastation are all around; blood runs deep throughout the city. Bodies are not even afforded the dignity of burial. Instead, they have been left on the streets, there to become carrion

II

5How long, LORD? Will you be
angry forever?
Will your jealous anger keep
burning like fire?
6Pour out your wrath on nations
that do not recognize you,
on kingdoms that do not call on
your name,
7For they have devoured Jacob,
laid waste his dwelling place.
8Do not remember against us the
iniquities of our forefathers;

let your compassion move
quickly ahead of us,
for we have been brought very
low.

III

9Help us, God our savior,
on account of the glory of your
name.
Deliver us, pardon our sins
for your name's sake.
10Why should the nations say,
"Where is their God?"

devoured by wild beasts and winged fowl. The people who prided themselves on being the chosen of God have become the butt of the mockery of neighboring nations. Comfort can be found nowhere.

5-7 The lament

The actual cry of lamentation opens in the traditional way: "How long, LORD?" Though the people suffer at the hands of others, they know that it is really God's wrath that they experience, a wrath that burns them like an unforgiving fire. This agonizing people pray that divine wrath might be turned away from them and toward their enemies. Despite the fact that these enemies have been instruments of God for the chastisement of Israel, they have wreaked havoc on the people of God and they have laid waste the land that was God's own heritage.

8-13 A prayer for release

The people acknowledge that they have been guilty of transgression. However, they pray that God's compassion might far exceed their culpability. Besides, they believe that the sufferings they have endured are punishment enough. Having called on the covenant characteristic of compassion, they now appeal to God's honor or reputation in the sight of the other nations. What would these nations think if God allowed this special people to be completely destroyed? Punishment for transgressions might be appropriate, but total destruction? Furthermore, these adversaries should not be able to gloat over the Israelite blood they have spilled. Such behavior might suggest that the God of Israel is powerless to act on behalf of the people.

▶ This symbol indicates a cross-reference number in the *Catechism of the Catholic Church*. See page 152 for number citations.

30

Before our eyes make known to the
nations
that you avenge the blood of
your servants which has
been poured out.

IV
¹¹Let the groaning of the imprisoned come in before you;
in accord with the greatness of
your arm
preserve those doomed to die.
¹²Turn back sevenfold into the
bosom of our neighbors
the insult with which they
insulted you, Lord.
¹³Then we, your people, the sheep
of your pasture,
will give thanks to you forever;

from generation to generation
we will recount your praise.

Prayer to Restore God's Vineyard

80 ¹For the leader; according to
"Lilies." *Eduth.* A psalm of Asaph.

I
²O Shepherd of Israel, lend an ear,
you who guide Joseph like a
flock!
Seated upon the cherubim, shine
forth
³upon Ephraim, Benjamin, and
Manasseh.
Stir up your power, and come to
save us.
⁴O God, restore us;
light up your face and we shall
be saved.

Modern sensibilities could be offended by the prayer for the affliction of enemies. Without condoning revenge, we must remember that such a petition is simply the reverse side of a prayer for victory in battle. This psalm clearly shows Israel's belief that its own enemies were also enemies of God. They would probably consider this a prayer for just punishment for their iniquities.

Psalm 80 (communal lament)

2-4 A cry to God

God is called on as shepherd and as warrior, two metaphors that capture the notion of divine protection. The throne among the cherubim could be a reference to God's heavenly throne, which was believed to be surrounded by angels, or to a shrine, before which representations of cherubim were commonly set up. Joseph, Ephraim, Benjamin, and Manasseh were northern tribes, suggesting a northern origin for the psalm. This section ends with a prayer (v. 4) that serves as a refrain throughout the psalm (cf. vv. 8, 20). In it the people ask for restoration and salvation.

5-8 The lament

The military title, "Lord of hosts," is followed by the traditional cry of lament: "how long?" God, who previously fought on behalf of the people now seems to be fighting against them, for their affliction has come from

II

⁵LORD of hosts,
  how long will you smolder in
    anger
  while your people pray?
⁶You have fed them the bread of
    tears,
  made them drink tears in great
    measure.
⁷You have left us to be fought over
    by our neighbors;
  our enemies deride us.
⁸O God of hosts, restore us;
  light up your face and we shall
    be saved.

III

⁹You brought a vine out of Egypt;
  you drove out nations and
    planted it.
¹⁰You cleared out what was before
    it;

it took deep root and filled the
    land.
¹¹The mountains were covered by
    its shadow,
  the cedars of God by its
    branches.
¹²It sent out its boughs as far as the
    sea,
  its shoots as far as the river.
¹³Why have you broken down its
    walls,
  so that all who pass along the
    way pluck its fruit?
¹⁴The boar from the forest strips the
    vine;
  the beast of the field feeds upon
    it.
¹⁵Turn back again, God of hosts;
  look down from heaven and see;
Visit this vine,
  ¹⁶the stock your right hand has
    planted,

---

the hand of God. They are forced to feed on sorrow as if it were food. Furthermore, now God has allowed warring neighbors to fight over the spoils of their defeat. This section ends, as did the first, with the same prayer for restoration and salvation.

9-20 Remember the blessings of the past

Prayers for deliverance are often rooted in remembrance of former blessings. Here God is reminded of the graciousness shown at the time of Israel's deliverance from Egypt and entrance into the land. Israel is characterized as a vine that was taken out of Egypt and transplanted in the land of promise. This vine grew larger and covered more territory than even mighty cedar trees—a reference to neighboring nations, specifically Lebanon. The sea (probably the Mediterranean) and the river (perhaps the Tigris or Euphrates) set the desired boundaries of Israel's land. Despite all of this care and magnificence, God allowed the nation to fall and the land to be overrun by wild animals.

Once again God is called on as the mighty "God of hosts" (v. 15) who has the power to save the people. The metaphor shifts back to that of a vine dresser: "Visit this vine." If God sees fit to restore this people, they will show their gratitude through praise and reverence. The man at God's right

and the son whom you made
  strong for yourself.
¹⁷Those who would burn or cut it
  down—
  may they perish at your rebuke.
¹⁸May your hand be with the man
  on your right,
  with the son of man whom you
    made strong for yourself.
¹⁹Then we will not withdraw from
  you;
  revive us, and we will call on
    your name.
²⁰LORD God of hosts, restore us;
  light up your face and we shall
    be saved.

An Admonition to Fidelity

81 ¹For the leader; "upon the *gittith.*"
  Of Asaph.

I

²Sing joyfully to God our strength;
  raise loud shouts to the God of
    Jacob!
³Take up a melody, sound the
  timbrel,
  the pleasant lyre with a harp.
⁴Blow the shofar at the new moon,
  at the full moon, on our solemn
    feast.
⁵For this is a law for Israel,
  an edict of the God of Jacob,
⁶He made it a decree for Joseph
  when he came out of the land of
    Egypt.

II

⁷I heard a tongue I did not know:
  "I removed his shoulder from
    the burden;

---

hand, the place of honor, is the king who is God's representative among the people. This third section ends with the refrain.

Psalm 81 (prophetic exhortation)

2-6b A call to praise

The liturgical elements of this call to praise are clear. The plural imperative form of the verbs suggests a joyful, even triumphant, community gathering: "Sing joyfully . . . / raise loud shouts." Singing to musical instruments is also directed. The sound of the trumpet (*shofar*) announced important liturgical commemorations such as the celebration of new moon, full moon, and solemn festivals. These celebrations were mandated by law (cf. Lev 23). The divine title "God of Jacob" and mention of the tribe of Joseph are usually associated with the northern tribes, suggesting a northern origin for the psalm.

6c-17 The oracle

The oracle from God consists of two reports: one of God's deliverance of the people from Egyptian bondage (vv. 7-11), the other of the people's rebellion in spite of God's graciousness (vv. 12-17).

Temple prophets frequently delivered an oracle from God as part of solemn temple liturgies. This is probably what is described here. The

his hands moved away from the basket."

⁸In distress you called and I rescued you;
   I answered you in secret with thunder;
At the waters of Meribah I tested you:

   Selah

⁹'Listen, my people, I will testify against you
   If only you will listen to me, Israel!
¹⁰There shall be no foreign god among you;
   you shall not bow down to an alien god.

¹¹I am the LORD your God,
   who brought you up from the land of Egypt.
   Open wide your mouth that I may fill it.'

¹²But my people did not listen to my words;
   Israel would not submit to me.
¹³So I thrust them away to the hardness of their heart;
   'Let them walk in their own machinations.'
¹⁴O that my people would listen to me,
   that Israel would walk in my ways,
¹⁵In a moment I would humble their foes,
   and turn back my hand against their oppressors.
¹⁶Those who hate the LORD will try flattering him,
   but their fate is fixed forever.
¹⁷But Israel I will feed with the finest wheat,
   I will satisfy them with honey from the rock."

---

images used in the description of the people's release from servitude capture the essence of their hard labor. They called and God responded. God not only rescued them but also cared for them in the wilderness when they had no other means of support. The mention of Meribah is a reminder of their infidelity in the wilderness (cf. Exod 17:1-7; Num 29:6-13). In the face of God's protective concern, the people's transgressions are baffling. The sin of the wilderness was murmuring against God, not idolatry. Therefore, the admonition against false worship was probably added at a later time. Some form of the phrase "I am the LORD your God," is a divine title that appears more than a hundred times in early traditions.

   For their part, the people refused to follow God's directions and so God abandoned them, allowing them to remain in their hardness of heart and to fall victim to the designs of dangerous enemies. Despite their sinfulness, however, God does not seem to be able to forsake forever this chosen people. If they return to God, God will once again defend them against their enemies. The oracle ends with the possibility of peace and prosperity. It is up to Israel to choose.

"Take up a melody, . . . the pleasant lyre with a harp. Blow the shofar at the new moon, . . ." (Ps 81:3-4).

The Downfall of Unjust Gods

82 ¹A psalm of Asaph.

I

God takes a stand in the divine council,
   gives judgment in the midst of the gods.
²"How long will you judge unjustly and favor the cause of the wicked?

Selah

³"Defend the lowly and fatherless;
   render justice to the afflicted and needy.
⁴Rescue the lowly and poor;
   deliver them from the hand of the wicked."

II

⁵The gods neither know nor understand,
   wandering about in darkness,
and all the world's foundations shake.
⁶I declare: "Gods though you be,
   offspring of the Most High all of you,

Psalm 82 (divine oracle)

I The divine council

The setting is the familiar ancient Near Eastern council of gods (cf. Job 1:6; 2:1). In Israelite tradition, Israel's own God is the mighty sovereign who reigns there. The presumed gods of the other nations are simply celestial bodies or the forces of nature created by God.

2-5 Divine directives

God chastises the members of the council for their failure to judge justly. The favoritism they show to the wicked may simply be the psalmist's way of describing the common understanding of the bias that patron gods show to their devotees. Instead of condemning the people for such worship, here God denounces the gods. They should have been attentive to the needy and those who are oppressed by the wicked. In other words, God is calling the members of the divine council to shift their own loyalties and to favor those whom the God of Israel favors. God moves from directly addressing the others gods to speaking about them (v. 5). Their lack of understanding does not merely affect them; it also threatens the very foundations of the earth.

6-8 Condemnation

There is some question about the identity of the speaker here. Some commentators claim that it could not be God, since the existence of other gods is not questioned. They maintain that it is the psalmist who, like other Israelites of the day, believed that other nations worshiped minor deities.

⁷Yet like any mortal you shall die;
  like any prince you shall fall."
⁸Arise, O God, judge the earth,
  for yours are all the nations.

Prayer Against a Hostile Alliance

83 ¹A song; a psalm of Asaph.

I

²God, do not be silent;
  God, do not be deaf or remain
    unmoved!
³See how your enemies rage;
  your foes proudly raise their
    heads.
⁴They conspire against your people,
  plot against those you protect.
⁵They say, "Come, let us wipe them
    out as a nation;
  let Israel's name be remembered
    no more!"
⁶They scheme with one mind,
  they have entered into a
    covenant against you:
⁷The tents of Edom and the
    Ishmaelites,
  of Moab and the Hagrites,
⁸Gebal, Ammon, and Amalek,
  Philistia and the inhabitants of
    Tyre.
⁹Assyria, too, in league with them,
  backs the descendants of Lot.

Selah

Whoever the speaker might be, the insignificance of these other gods is underscored. Like human beings, they are transient and have no enduring future.

The final verse is a prayer to God, and it clearly comes from the psalmist. To ask God to judge the earth is to acknowledge God's universal sovereignty, even over those gods to whom other nations look for protection and justice.

Psalm 83 (communal lament)

2-9 Lament

The people pray that God will step in and end the persecution that they are suffering at the hands of those who are identified as God's own enemies. These foes are so identified because they are enemies of God's people. They have conspired to destroy this people so completely that not even their memory will endure. For people who did not have a well-defined belief in life after this life, to be blotted out of memory was considered the ultimate threat. It would be as if one had never even existed. Conspiracy against God's people was conspiracy against God. The nations named were those neighbors who at some time in their history warred against Israel. Ishmael, born of the Egyptian Hagar, and the rival brother of Isaac, was associated with the Transjordanian country of Edom (cf. Gen 25:22-26), the nation that much later forbade the Israelite people from passing through it on their way to the land of promise (cf. Num 20:18). The Hagrites, probably linked

II

¹⁰Deal with them as with Midian;
   as with Sisera and Jabin at the
     wadi Kishon,
¹¹Those destroyed at Endor,
   who became dung for the
     ground.
¹²Make their nobles like Oreb and
   Zeeb,
   all their princes like Zebah and
     Zalmunna,
¹³Who made a plan together,
   "Let us take for ourselves the
     pastures of God."
¹⁴My God, make them like
   tumbleweed,

into chaff flying before the wind.
¹⁵As a fire raging through a forest,
   a flame setting mountains
     ablaze,
¹⁶Pursue them with your tempest;
   terrify them with your storm-
     wind.
¹⁷Cover their faces with shame,
   till they seek your name, LORD.
¹⁸Let them be ashamed and terrified
   forever;
   let them perish in disgrace.
¹⁹Let them know that your name is
   LORD,
   you alone are the Most High
     over all the earth.

---

with Hagar, also lived east of the Jordan. Gebal was near Petra in the east; Ammon and Amalek were also eastern nations. Only Philistia (cf. Josh 13:3) and Tyre (cf. Ezek 26:3) were to the west of Israel. The most threatening nation was Assyria, the superpower to the northeast (cf. 2 Kgs 17:6).

10-19 Prayers for redress

Those who oppressed the chosen people of God have also sinned against God and should be punished. They should be punished just as earlier nations that had similarly transgressed were smitten by the righteous wrath of God. The Midianites were a desert people who constituted a serious threat during the time that Israel was settling in the land. Zebah and Zalmunna were kings of that nation (cf. Judg 8:6), and Oreb and Zeeb were princes (cf. Judg 7:25). Under Gideon's leadership they were conquered. The Canaanite king Jabin and his general Sisera were defeated at the time of the judges (cf. Judg 4), as was the territory of Endor (cf. Josh 17:11).

The people pray that afflictions will devastate their adversaries. The enemies sought to erase from memory the name of Israel. Now Israel asks that those same enemies be withered up and blown away, or burned to ashes. In either case, nothing would remain of them and so they would be forgotten. They pray for terror and shame, for battles could be won because of terror, and shame is sometimes even worse than death. What the people are really asking is that the sovereign power of God be made manifest in the defeat of their and God's enemies.

Prayer of a Pilgrim to Jerusalem

84 ¹For the leader; "upon the *gittith*."
A psalm of the Korahites.

I

²How lovely your dwelling,
O LORD of hosts!
³My soul yearns and pines
for the courts of the LORD.
My heart and flesh cry out
for the living God.
⁴As the sparrow finds a home
and the swallow a nest to settle
her young,
My home is by your altars,
LORD of hosts, my king and my
God!

⁵Blessed are those who dwell in
your house!
They never cease to praise you.

Selah

II

⁶Blessed the man who finds refuge
in you,
in their hearts are pilgrim roads.
⁷As they pass through the Baca
valley,
they find spring water to drink.
The early rain covers it with
blessings.
⁸They will go from strength to
strength
and see the God of gods on
Zion.

Psalm 84 (song of Zion)

2-5 Happiness in the temple

In this psalm, devotion toward God extends to an overwhelming attachment to the house of God, the place on earth where God dwells in the midst of the people in a very special way. The yearning of the psalmist indicates distance from the temple at this time. This yearning is all-encompassing, affecting both body and inner being. Though the desired sense of security, which is compared with that experienced by nesting birds, introduces the idea of protection from harm, the overriding sentiments here are those of intimacy and serenity. The military designation "LORD of hosts" is softened somewhat by the reference "living God." The section ends with a beatitude "Blessed!" Those who dwell in God's presence are certainly happy or blessed.

6-8 Diving protection

This second section opens with a macarism. Here the focus shifts from the tranquility associated with God's presence to the divine protection that it guarantees. The picture sketched is that of a pilgrimage. Commentators have been unable to locate the Baca valley. The derivation of the word ("to weep," thus yielding "valley of tears"), along with the mention of God's gift of water, has led some to conclude that this is a reference to an arid stretch of land through which the people passed on their way to Jerusalem. It could also be a figurative way of describing the interior movement from

III

⁹Lᴏʀᴅ God of hosts, hear my
    prayer;
    listen, God of Jacob.

Selah

¹⁰O God, watch over our shield;
    look upon the face of your
    anointed.

IV

¹¹Better one day in your courts
    than a thousand elsewhere.
Better the threshold of the house of
    my God
    than a home in the tents of the
    wicked.

¹²For a sun and shield is the Lᴏʀᴅ
    God,
    bestowing all grace and glory.
The Lᴏʀᴅ withholds no good thing
    from those who walk without
    reproach.
¹³O Lᴏʀᴅ of hosts,
    blessed the man who trusts in
    you!

Prayer for Divine Favor

85 ¹For the leader. A psalm of the
    Korahites.

I

²You once favored, Lᴏʀᴅ, your land,
    restored the captives of Jacob.

---

thirsting for God's presence to enjoying the refreshment that experiencing
that presence ultimately brings.

9-10 A prayer for the king

The military tone of these verses is seen in the divine epithet "Lᴏʀᴅ of
hosts" and in the characterization of the king as the shield of the people.
The focus here is on protection, not aggression.

11-13 Delight in the presence of God

The psalmist includes two examples of "better than" proverbs in this
praise of the temple. The comparisons may seem exaggerated, but they
clearly convey the high regard in which are held the temple itself and time
spent within the temple. God protects ("shield") the righteous and provides
everything ("sun") that is necessary for prosperous life. The psalm ends
with a macarism that exhorts trust in God. The frequent use of "Lᴏʀᴅ of
hosts" (four times) testifies to the divine power that inspires such trust.

Psalm 85 (communal lament)

2-4 Remember the past

Speaking in the name of the people, the psalmist reminds God of some
of the favors they enjoyed in the past. This is done in order to encourage
God to grant similar favors in the present. The verb "restore" became a
technical term referring to the restoration of the nation after the Babylonian
exile. This seems to be the sense of the psalm here. Since the exile was

³You forgave the guilt of your
    people,
  pardoned all their sins.

                              Selah

⁴You withdrew all your wrath,
    turned back from your burning
      anger.

                    II

⁵Restore us, God of our salvation;
    let go of your displeasure with
      us.
⁶Will you be angry with us forever,
    prolong your anger for all
      generations?
⁷Certainly you will again restore
    our life,
    that your people may rejoice in
      you.

⁸Show us, LORD, your mercy;
    grant us your salvation.

                    III

⁹I will listen for what God, the
      LORD, has to say;
    surely he will speak of peace
  To his people and to his faithful.
    May they not turn to foolishness!
¹⁰Near indeed is his salvation for
      those who fear him;
    glory will dwell in our land.
¹¹Love and truth will meet;
    justice and peace will kiss.
¹²Truth will spring from the earth;
    justice will look down from
      heaven.
¹³Yes, the LORD will grant his bounty;
    our land will yield its produce.
¹⁴Justice will march before him,
    and make a way for his footsteps.

perceived as punishment for the sins of the people, their restoration would have been viewed as evidence of divine forgiveness, pardon, withdrawal of wrath, and turning back of anger.

5-8 Prayer for deliverance

The prayer is now explicit. Though specifics are not given regarding the situation within which the people now find themselves, they are definitely suffering. The psalmist would not speak of divine wrath if this were not the case, for Israel believed that misfortune was God's angry response to their infidelity. The prayer is fourfold: "Restore us . . . / restore our life . . . / Show us, LORD, your mercy; / grant us your salvation." The people bring these prayers to God, who is the savior from whom alone salvation will come.

9-14 Trust in God's graciousness

After past favors have been recalled and petitions for deliverance have been offered, the graciousness of God is praised. For the only time in this psalm, the psalmist speaks as an individual, as one who is confident that God will respond favorably to the people's prayer. In this trust, the psalmist waits for God's word of assurance. The role that the psalmist plays in the prayer of the people prompts some commentators to conclude that the setting is liturgical, the people having brought their needs to worship, with

Prayer in Time of Distress

86 ¹A prayer of David.

I

Incline your ear, Lord, and answer
  me,
  for I am poor and oppressed.
²Preserve my life, for I am devoted;
  save your servant who trusts in
    you.
You are my God; ³be gracious to
  me, Lord;
  to you I call all the day.
⁴Gladden the soul of your servant;
  to you, Lord, I lift up my soul.
⁵Lord, you are good and forgiving,
  most merciful to all who call on
    you.

⁶Lord, hear my prayer;
  listen to my cry for help.
⁷On the day of my distress I call to
    you,
  for you will answer me.

II

⁸None among the gods can equal
    you, O Lord;
  nor can their deeds compare to
    yours.
⁹All the nations you have made
    shall come
  to bow before you, Lord,
  and give honor to your name.
¹⁰For you are great and do
    wondrous deeds;
  and you alone are God.

---

the psalmist acting as mediator between them and God. God's forgiving response depends on their repentance and promise of future faithfulness. Reconciliation with God results in the restoration of characteristics of the covenant bond that had been fractured by the people's sin: love, truth, justice, peace (*shalom*). God's good favor will be seen in the eventual prosperity that will surround the forgiven people.

Psalm 86 (lament of an individual)

1b-7 A call for help

The psalm opens with a series of petitions: "Incline your ear . . . answer . . . / Preserve . . . / save . . . be gracious . . . / Gladden . . . / hear . . . / listen." The psalmist claims to be a faithful covenant partner, and so this suffering is not punishment for sin. Rather, it is oppression caused by enemies, and God is called on to intervene. Although this section of the psalm is replete with petition, the tone of the prayers and the way God is portrayed subtly show that the psalmist perceives God as faithful and concerned about the welfare of the righteous. This is confirmed by the unflinching trust expressed in the psalm (v. 7).

8-10 Praise of God

The people of Israel worshiped only one God, but they did not always reject the possibility that other nations had their own gods. Even when they

III

[11]Teach me, Lord, your way
   that I may walk in your truth,
   single-hearted and revering
      your name.
[12]I will praise you with all my heart,
   glorify your name forever, Lord
      my God.
[13]Your mercy to me is great;
   you have rescued me from the
      depths of Sheol.
[14]O God, the arrogant have risen
      against me;
   a ruthless band has sought my
      life;
to you they pay no heed.
[15]But you, Lord, are a compassionate
      and gracious God,
   slow to anger, abounding in
      mercy and truth.
[16]Turn to me, be gracious to me;
   give your strength to your
      servant;
   save the son of your handmaid.
[17]Give me a sign of your favor:
   make my enemies see, to their
      confusion,
   that you, Lord, help and
      comfort me.

---

entertained this idea, they insisted that their God was superior to all other deities, being the maker of all that was created. Furthermore, they maintained that eventually other nations would recognize their God's superiority, would switch their allegiance, and would join them in paying homage to the Lord who was really the only true God.

11-17 Petitions repeated

A second set of petitions is directed toward God. Some of them repeat preceding sentiments, others do not. The first prayer arises from the wisdom tradition, which exhorts the student to choose one way of life over another. The psalmist prays for instruction in God's way, the way of truth and commitment to righteousness. With this kind of training, the psalmist would be able to praise God's name appropriately. There is no explicit expression of thanksgiving; however, the acknowledgment of divine covenant love that prompted God to rescue the psalmist from some dimension of death (Sheol) certainly lays the ground for sentiments of gratitude. Those who rise up against the psalmist are identified as enemies of God. Therefore, any defense of the psalmist would be a defense of God's honor. What the psalmist seeks is the downfall of these enemies. Their defeat will be seen as a victory for God and a sign of God's partiality toward the psalmist. Once again, covenant language is used to represent God: merciful and gracious, loving and true. God is characterized in this same way in the Exodus tradition after the people had sinned with the golden calf (cf. Exod 34:6). This phrase became one of the standard ways of describing God.

Zion the True Birthplace

87 ¹A psalm of the Korahites. A song.

I

His foundation is on holy
   mountains,
²The LORD loves the gates of Zion
   more than any dwelling in
   Jacob.
³Glorious things are said of you,
   O city of God!

Selah

II

⁴Rahab and Babylon I count
   among those who know me.
See, Philistia and Tyre, with
   Ethiopia,
   "This one was born there."
⁵And of Zion it will be said:
   "Each one was born in it."
The Most High will establish it;
   ⁶the LORD notes in the register of
   the peoples:
   "This one was born there."

Selah

⁷So singers and dancers:
   "All my springs are in you."

Psalm 87 (song of Zion)

1-3 Jerusalem, the favored city

It is not uncommon that Israelites insist that Zion far exceeds in grandeur the cities of other nations. Here it is said to be more loved by God than any other Israelite city. In fact, it is God's own city, built on a high mountain so that all can see it and marvel at its splendor. The superiority of this city, also known as the city of David, could be a way of asserting God's preference for that southern king and all his descendants.

4-7 Jerusalem, the mother of the people

Cities were frequently personified as mothers of the inhabitants within them. Such a familial relationship with Jerusalem is here extended to others as well. The boundaries of this influence are remarkable. Babylon and Egypt (the Hebrew has Rahab, the mythological monster associated with Egypt [cf. Isa 30:7]) were the ancient and somewhat distant superpowers that set the general geographic boundaries of the ancient Near East. Philistia, Ethiopia, and Tyre were smaller nations immediately adjacent to Israel. Some commentators maintain that the psalmist is speaking about Jews living in Diaspora in these nations. They would certainly have claimed citizenship. Others think that the reference is to natives of these nations who had chosen the Lord as their God. Their membership would have been religious. Whoever these people might have been, the sense of the psalm is quite clear—there are people outside the geographic boundaries of Israel who claim Zion as their city and pay homage to its God.

A Despairing Lament

88 ¹A song; a psalm of the Korahites. For the leader; according to *Mahalath*. For singing; a *maskil* of Heman the Ezrahite.

I

²Lord, the God of my salvation, I
    call out by day;
    at night I cry aloud in your
      presence.
³Let my prayer come before you;
    incline your ear to my cry.
⁴For my soul is filled with troubles;
    my life draws near to Sheol.
⁵I am reckoned with those who go
      down to the pit;
    I am like a warrior without
      strength.

⁶My couch is among the dead,
    like the slain who lie in the
      grave.
You remember them no more;
    they are cut off from your
      influence.
⁷You plunge me into the bottom of
      the pit,
    into the darkness of the abyss.
⁸Your wrath lies heavy upon me;
    all your waves crash over me.

Selah

II

⁹Because of you my acquaintances
    shun me;
    you make me loathsome to
      them;
Caged in, I cannot escape;

Psalm 88 (lament of an individual)

2-3 The lament

Day and night cries for help rise to God. Loud cries suggest unrelenting anguish. The fact that pleas are made at all suggests a degree of trust in God. However, there is still a sense of foreboding here, as if God might not listen after all.

4-10 The psalmist's affliction

Sheol, the pit, and the abyss are references to the place of the dead. Israel did not believe in utter annihilation after death, but neither did it have a well-developed idea of life after this life. Therefore, Sheol was not considered a place of punishment. Israel dreaded it, not because of what happened to the dead when they were there, but because of the death that brought them there in the first place. Affliction of any kind was considered a foretaste of ultimate death. Therefore, the one who was in any way suffering was thought to be struggling with death itself.

Suffering was also ascribed to divine wrath, God's anger in the face of transgression. It crashed upon the tormented one like a series of waves cascading upon the shore. Unfortunately, people often tend to avoid those who are suffering, perhaps because suffering is so hard to witness, or because those who would like to help frequently feel so powerless before it.

¹⁰my eyes grow dim from
trouble.
All day I call on you, LORD;
I stretch out my hands to you.
¹¹Do you work wonders for the
dead?
Do the shades arise and praise
you?

Selah

III

¹²Is your mercy proclaimed in the
grave,
your faithfulness among those
who have perished?
¹³Are your marvels declared in the
darkness,
your righteous deeds in the land
of oblivion?

IV

¹⁴But I cry out to you, LORD;
in the morning my prayer
comes before you.
¹⁵Why do you reject my soul, LORD,
and hide your face from me?
¹⁶I have been mortally afflicted
since youth;
I have borne your terrors and I
am made numb.
¹⁷Your wrath has swept over me;
your terrors have destroyed me.
¹⁸All day they surge round like a
flood;
from every side they encircle
me.
¹⁹Because of you friend and neighbor
shun me;
my only friend is darkness.

If it is punishment from God, then the one suffering will also have to endure the shame that accompanies culpability. All of this explains the sense of revulsion many experience in the face of suffering. Unfortunately, the one suffering is unable to escape.

11-13 God is questioned

The psalmist addresses a series of rhetorical questions to God. Besides underscoring the futility of suffering, Israel's understanding of the nether-world is revealed. At this point in its history, Israel did not believe that God's jurisdiction extended into the world of the dead. God's power was not felt there, nor did those who dwelt there praise God. In other words, the God of Israel was revered as the God of the living, not of the dead.

14-19 Lament repeated

The cries of lament are repeated. The silence from God is interpreted as rejection. Affliction includes many of the signs of death, and the psalmist has endured this for a prolonged period of time. Furthermore, those who should support the tortured individual have turned their backs. Abandoned by all, the only companion is darkness. The psalm ends with not even a hint of hope.

A Lament over God's Promise to David

▲ *89* ¹A *maskil* of Ethan the Ezrahite.

A

I

²I will sing of your mercy forever,
LORD
proclaim your faithfulness
through all ages.
³For I said, "My mercy is established
forever;
my faithfulness will stand as
long as the heavens.
⁴I have made a covenant with my
chosen one;
I have sworn to David my
servant:

⁵I will make your dynasty stand
forever
and establish your throne
through all ages."

Selah

II

⁶The heavens praise your marvels,
LORD,
your loyalty in the assembly of
the holy ones.
⁷Who in the skies ranks with the
LORD?
Who is like the LORD among the
sons of the gods?
⁸A God dreaded in the council of
the holy ones,
greater and more awesome than
all those around him!
⁹LORD, God of hosts, who is like
you?

Psalm 89 (royal psalm)

2-5 A royal covenant

The psalm opens with a hymn in praise of God who promised to make a covenant with the royal house of David and who has been faithful to that promise. The promise was prompted by God's love and faithfulness. Just as that faithfulness is enduring, so will this covenant last throughout the ages.

6-19 Praise of the creator

The scene reflects the ancient Near Eastern council of the gods. What other nations revered as minor deities, Israel considered created celestial beings. These creatures offer their homage to the Lord God of hosts, the one who rules over all other gods. The description is of the primeval cosmic battle in which God was triumphant over the forces of chaotic waters. Rahab is the name given to the monster of the deep (cf. Job 26:12; Isa 51:9). The orderly universe was established after the battle had been won.

The scene moves from the heavens to earth, from myth to the ancient world. Zaphon was the sacred mountain on which the Canaanite god Baal was believed to dwell; Amanus is a mountain in southern Turkey; Tabor

47

Mighty LORD, your faithfulness
surrounds you.
[10]You rule the raging sea;
you still its swelling waves.
[11]You crush Rahab with a mortal
blow;
with your strong arm you
scatter your foes.
[12]Yours are the heavens, yours the
earth;
you founded the world and
everything in it.
[13]Zaphon and Amanus you created;
Tabor and Hermon rejoice in
your name.
[14]You have a mighty arm.
Your hand is strong; your right
hand is ever exalted.
[15]Justice and judgment are the
foundation of your throne;
mercy and faithfulness march
before you.
[16]Blessed the people who know the
war cry,
who walk in the radiance of
your face, LORD.
[17]In your name they sing joyfully all
the day;
they rejoice in your
righteousness.

[18]You are their majestic strength;
by your favor our horn is
exalted.
[19]Truly the LORD is our shield,
the Holy One of Israel, our king!

III

[20]Then you spoke in vision;
to your faithful ones you said:
"I have set a leader over the
warriors;
I have raised up a chosen one
from the people.
[21]I have chosen David, my servant;
with my holy oil I have anointed
him.
[22]My hand will be with him;
my arm will make him strong.
[23]No enemy shall outwit him,
nor shall the wicked defeat him.
[24]I will crush his foes before him,
strike down those who hate
him.
[25]My faithfulness and mercy will be
with him;
through my name his horn will
be exalted.
[26]I will set his hand upon the sea,
his right hand upon the rivers.

and Hermon are found in Israel itself. These mountains, majestic peaks that inspired wonder and religious devotion in the people, now praise the God who fashioned them. God's own royal rule is extolled, a rule founded in righteousness and justice. Those who recognize and acclaim this rule are called "Blessed." By deftly drawing a line from primeval victory through the marvels of creation to the rule over the people, the psalmist has shown that the cosmic conqueror and creator of all is none other than the God of Israel.

20-38 The divine oracle

God speaks and briefly recounts the choice of David as commander of Israel's armies and king over all the people (cf. 1 Sam 16:1-3; 2 Sam 7:11-16). The faithfulness and love that were lauded earlier (v. 3) were bestowed in

²⁷He shall cry to me, 'You are my
father,
my God, the Rock of my
salvation!'
²⁸I myself make him the firstborn,
Most High over the kings of the
earth.
²⁹Forever I will maintain my mercy
for him;
my covenant with him stands
firm.
³⁰I will establish his dynasty forever,
his throne as the days of the
heavens.
³¹If his descendants forsake my
teaching,
do not follow my decrees,
³²If they fail to observe my statutes,
do not keep my commandments,
³³I will punish their crime with a
rod
and their guilt with blows.
³⁴But I will not take my mercy from
him,

nor will I betray my bond of
faithfulness.
³⁵I will not violate my covenant;
the promise of my lips I will not
alter.
³⁶By my holiness I swore once for
all:
I will never be false to David.
³⁷His dynasty will continue forever,
his throne, like the sun before
me.
³⁸Like the moon it will stand eternal,
forever firm like the sky!"

Selah

B

IV
³⁹But now you have rejected and
spurned,
been enraged at your anointed.
⁴⁰You renounced the covenant with
your servant,
defiled his crown in the dust.

---

a special way on David (v. 25). He will be given rule over the unruly sea
and rivers, making him the mightiest ruler of the earth, actually wielding
some of the power that belonged to the divine warrior. Many ancient people
believed that their king was a direct descendant of their god. Israel retained
elements of that royal ideology, but reinterpreted them. The king did have
a kind of father-son relationship with God, but it was one of responsibility,
not descent. Though the Davidic dynasty was afforded divine legitimation,
its human character is also clearly stated in the psalm. All Israelites, even
the kings, were bound by the regulations of the law. All violators would
have been punished, including the kings. The promise of the dynasty's
enduring rule is firmly rooted in the establishment of cosmic order. It will
last forever, like the sun and the moon.

39-52 Lament over the ruin of the king

Included in the royal covenant was the king's responsibility to uphold
the law. What follows is an account of the afflictions that befell him when
he was not faithful to that responsibility. Just as throughout this psalm
"David" represents the dynasty generally and not merely the specific man,

⁴¹You broke down all city walls,
    left his strongholds in ruins.
⁴²All who pass through seize
    plunder;
    his neighbors deride him.
⁴³You have exalted the right hand of
    his foes,
    have gladdened all his enemies.
⁴⁴You turned back his sharp sword,
    did not support him in battle.
⁴⁵You brought to an end his
    splendor,
    hurled his throne to the ground.
⁴⁶You cut short the days of his
    youth,
    covered him with shame.

Selah

V

⁴⁷How long, LORD? Will you hide
    forever?
    Must your wrath smolder like
    fire?

⁴⁸Remember how brief life is,
    how frail the sons of man you
    have created!
⁴⁹What is man, that he should live
    and not see death?
    Who can deliver his soul from
    the power of Sheol?

Selah

VI

⁵⁰Where are your former mercies,
    Lord,
    that you swore to David in your
    faithfulness?
⁵¹Remember, Lord, the insults to
    your servants,
    how I have borne in my bosom
    the slander of the nations.
⁵²Your enemies, LORD, insult;
    they insult each step of your
    anointed.
⁵³Blessed be the LORD forever!
    Amen and amen!

---

so these verses might contain a description of the failure of any of the kings. The report of ruined strongholds and the collapse of royal rule (vv. 41-45) lead some to believe that the reference is to the exile. God originally warned the kings that they would pay for their sinfulness by defeat at the hands of their enemies (cf. 2 Sam 7:14-15). That warning was not heeded and so calamity struck.

The psalmist cries out in typical lament fashion: "How long?" How long will God remain hidden? How long will divine anger rule the day? Human frailty is used as an incentive for divine forbearance. God made human beings weak: how can God expect more from them? The psalmist next appeals to the promises made to David. Even though the kings have been unfaithful, surely God will remain constant. The psalm ends on that note.

53 Doxology

The last verse is less a resolution of the sentiments of this psalm than it is the conclusion of the entire third book. Though shorter, it resembles similar conclusions of the previous books (cf. Pss 41:14; 72:18-20).

Fourth Book—Psalms 90–106

God's Eternity and Human Frailty

90 ¹A prayer of Moses, the man of God.

I

Lord, you have been our refuge
     through all generations.
²Before the mountains were born,
     the earth and the world brought
          forth,
     from eternity to eternity you are
          God.
³You turn humanity back into dust,
     saying, "Return, you children of
          Adam!"
⁴A thousand years in your eyes
     are merely a day gone by,
Before a watch passes in the night,
     ⁵you wash them away;

They sleep,
     and in the morning they sprout
          again like an herb.
⁶In the morning it blooms only to
          pass away;
     in the evening it is wilted and
          withered.

II

⁷Truly we are consumed by your
          anger,
     filled with terror by your wrath.
⁸You have kept our faults before
          you,
     our hidden sins in the light of
          your face.
⁹Our life ebbs away under your
          wrath;
     our years end like a sigh.
¹⁰Seventy is the sum of our years,
     or eighty, if we are strong;

BOOK FOUR: PSALMS 90–106

Psalm 90 (communal lament)

1b-6 The fleeting nature of human life

(This is the only psalm attributed to Moses.) The psalm opens with words of praise. God, who existed before all of creation, is acclaimed the everlasting God. What human beings would consider incalculable periods of time are as nothing to the God of all eternity. The fleeting nature of human life is compared to the short four-hour duration of a night watch. Human mortality, which is associated with the dust of death (cf. Gen 3:19), is compared to the daylong lifespan of grass. The themes of this first part of the prayer are reminiscent of wisdom teaching on the transitory nature of human life and its perishability (cf. Job 14:2).

7-11 Divine punishment

God's anger is fierce, like a consuming fire. It is also unrelenting, a fury that the people have brought on by their own sins. In the first verses of the psalm, the psalmist lamented the fleeting nature of life. A different perspective is expressed here. A longer life is also troublesome because it is usually

Most of them are toil and sorrow;
  they pass quickly, and we are
    gone.
[11]Who comprehends the strength of
    your anger?
  Your wrath matches the fear it
    inspires.
[12]Teach us to count our days aright,
  that we may gain wisdom of
    heart.

III

[13]Relent, O Lord! How long?
  Have pity on your servants!
[14]Fill us at daybreak with your
    mercy,
  that all our days we may sing
    for joy.
[15]Make us glad as many days as
  you humbled us,

for as many years as we have
    seen trouble.
[16]Show your deeds to your servants,
  your glory to their children.
[17]May the favor of the Lord our
    God be ours.
  Prosper the work of our hands!
  Prosper the work of our hands!

Security Under God's Protection

91

I

[1]You who dwell in the shelter of the
    Most High,
  who abide in the shade of the
    Almighty,
[2]Say to the Lord, "My refuge and
    fortress,
  my God in whom I trust."

---

filled with trouble and wearisome toil (cf. Job 7:1). In other words, life itself is a burden, regardless of its duration.

12-17 Prayers of petition

The psalm ends with a collection of prayers. The first plea is for wisdom. Several theological concepts are brought together in the second prayer. It asks God to "Relent," the traditional word for "change one's heart." This is followed by the familiar cry of lament: "How long?" Appeal is then made to the covenant features of mercy and steadfast love. The psalmist asks that the people be granted as many days of happiness as they have been forced to endure in affliction. In these prayers for restoration, the people are called God's servant, God's children—references to the covenant relationship. The final prayer is a general request for divine favor.

Psalm 91 (prayer of confidence of an individual)

1-2 God, a sure refuge

Two well-known names for God illustrate the role that God plays in this psalm. "Most High" is the title attributed to the original deity worshiped in Jerusalem and then appropriated to the God of Israel once David captured that city (cf. Gen 14:18). This high God provides a shelter in which one can find safety. "Almighty," the divine epithet of the patron God of

³He will rescue you from the
fowler's snare,
from the destroying plague,
⁴He will shelter you with his pinions,
and under his wings you may
take refuge;
his faithfulness is a protecting
shield.
⁵You shall not fear the terror of the
night
nor the arrow that flies by day,
⁶Nor the pestilence that roams in
darkness,
nor the plague that ravages at
noon.
⁷Though a thousand fall at your
side,
ten thousand at your right hand,
near you it shall not come.
⁸You need simply watch;
the punishment of the wicked
you will see.
⁹Because you have the LORD for
your refuge

and have made the Most High
your stronghold,
¹⁰No evil shall befall you,   ▶
no affliction come near your
tent.
¹¹For he commands his angels with   ▶
regard to you,
to guard you wherever you go.
¹²With their hands they shall   ▶
support you,
lest you strike your foot against
a stone.
¹³You can tread upon the asp and   ▶
the viper,
trample the lion and the dragon.

II

¹⁴Because he clings to me I will
deliver him;
because he knows my name I
will set him on high.
¹⁵He will call upon me and I will
answer;
I will be with him in distress;

Abram (cf. Gen 17:1), emphasizes God's superiority. In this psalm, this title too is associated with security. Both names signify that under the protection of the supreme God, one has nothing to fear. God is further described as refuge and fortress, two more references to security. By attributing to God these four titles, the psalmist means to generate trust in God.

3-13 Divine protection

The psalmist encourages an unnamed listener to trust in God. The troubles of which the psalmist speaks are depicted in various ways: a snare, the plague, darkness, deadly weapons. In each case, God will intervene and either ward off the attacks or release the afflicted one from distress. Covenant faithfulness (v. 4) is lifted up as a trustworthy defense. Others may fall victim to these assaults, but whoever trusts in God the Most High will be spared. God's protection is administered through angels who ward off all forms of danger (vv. 11-12). (This passage may have influenced our understanding of guardian angels.) Asp, viper, lion, and dragon denote dangerous animals, or they could be metaphors for threatening enemies.

I will deliver him and give him
honor.
¹⁶With length of days I will satisfy
him,
and fill him with my saving
power.

A Hymn of Thanksgiving for God's Fidelity

92 ¹A psalm. A sabbath song.

I

²It is good to give thanks to the
LORD,
to sing praise to your name,
Most High,
³To proclaim your love at daybreak,
your faithfulness in the night,
⁴With the ten-stringed harp,
with melody upon the lyre.

⁵For you make me jubilant, LORD,
by your deeds;
at the works of your hands I
shout for joy.

II

⁶How great are your works, LORD!
How profound your designs!
⁷A senseless person cannot know
this;
a fool cannot comprehend.
⁸Though the wicked flourish like
grass
and all sinners thrive,
They are destined for eternal
destruction;
⁹but you, LORD, are forever on
high.
¹⁰Indeed your enemies, LORD,
indeed your enemies shall perish;
all sinners shall be scattered.

14-16 God speaks

God promises to stand by all who are faithful and who honor the divine name. Since the name represents part of one's essence, to honor God's name is to honor God. Those who do so will enjoy divine protection. God will be their deliverer and will act as savior on their behalf.

Psalm 92 (prayer of thanksgiving of an individual)

2-4 Give thanks to God

The psalm opens with what appears to be a call to others to give thanks to God. It then moves immediately to a proclamation of praise directed to God. Such praise is appropriate all day long, both morning and evening. Reference to musical instruments suggests liturgical performance.

5-12 Reasons for gratitude

The "deeds" and "works of your hands," for which the psalmist is grateful, could be a reference to the wonders of creation or blessings that Israel experienced within its own history. If one interprets them from the context of the rest of the psalm, one could say that they refer to the justice that God will exact on Israel's enemies and the subsequent punishment meted out to them.

III

[11]You have given me the strength of a wild ox;
you have poured rich oil upon me.
[12]My eyes look with glee on my wicked enemies;
my ears shall hear what happens to my wicked foes.
[13]The just shall flourish like the palm tree,
shall grow like a cedar of Lebanon.
[14]Planted in the house of the LORD,
they shall flourish in the courts of our God.
[15]They shall bear fruit even in old age,
they will stay fresh and green,
[16]To proclaim: "The LORD is just;
my rock, in whom there is no wrong."

God Is a Mighty King

93 [1]The LORD is king, robed with majesty;
the LORD is robed, girded with might.

"Works" is in a parallel construction with "designs" (also translated "thought" or "device"). This suggests the wisdom tradition rather than history. God's purposes are not comprehended by fools and, therefore, the foolish will suffer the consequences of their foolishness. In the wisdom tradition, there is a very thin line between folly and sin. The psalmist crosses that line here. Sinners may think that they will escape punishment, but their good fortune will not last (short-lived like grass); retribution will ultimately overtake them.

The psalmist, on the other hand, is certain of God's favor. The Hebrew word translated "strength" is really "horn," a symbol of power; anointing with rich oil suggests extravagant blessing. The psalmist takes great delight in personal blessing as well as the downfall of the wicked.

13-16 The reward of the righteous

Nature metaphors are used to describe the blessings that the just will enjoy. Palm trees produce dates that are a staple in the diet of the Near East. The cedars of Lebanon were famous for their majesty. Wood from these trees was used to construct the temple. The righteous are said to be like these trees, established in the courts of God and bearing fruit for many years.

The psalm ends with a joyful shout of praise of God who is just and reliable.

Psalm 93 (kingship of God)

1-5 The majesty of the divine king

The psalm opens with what might be considered a shout of acclamation. "The LORD is king"—and no one else is! Both the shout and the scene

The world will surely stand in
place,
  never to be moved.
[2]Your throne stands firm from of
old;
  you are from everlasting.
[3]The flood has raised up, LORD;
  the flood has raised up its roar;
  the flood has raised its pounding
    waves.
[4]More powerful than the roar of
many waters,
  more powerful than the break-
    ers of the sea,
  powerful in the heavens is the
    LORD.
[5]Your decrees are firmly established;
  holiness befits your house,
    LORD,
  for all the length of days.

A Prayer for Deliverance from the Wicked

94

I

[1]LORD, avenging God,
  avenging God, shine forth!
[2]Rise up, O judge of the earth;
  give the proud what they
    deserve!

II

[3]How long, LORD, shall the wicked,
  how long shall the wicked glory?
[4]How long will they mouth
    haughty speeches,
  go on boasting, all these
    evildoers?
[5]They crush your people, LORD,
  torment your very own.

---

described originated in a mythological account of the primordial chaos battle (cf. Ps 89:10-12). After this battle was won, a palace was constructed in the heavens for the conqueror, and a throne was set up. From there, the victorious king rules over all. The unruly waters were tamed during the battle and are no longer a threat to the order of the cosmos. God's rule extends to the earth as well. The one who ordered the heavens also established laws to be followed on earth. Furthermore, God's heavenly dwelling is mirrored in God's holy temple on earth.

Psalm 94 (communal lament)

1-2 A cry for retribution

The psalm opens with words that are quite jarring for those who think of God as being primarily gentle and merciful. However, God is also just, and the psalmist is calling on that justice to right the wrongs that have been committed against God's people and, therefore, against God. It is important to note that the psalmist acknowledges that justice and vengeance will be meted out by God (cf. Deut 32:35) and not by vindictive human beings.

3-7 The deeds of the wicked

The lament itself begins with the standard cry of complaint: "How long?" The sinners take pride in their sins; they even boast about them.

"The just shall flourish like the palm tree, shall grow like a cedar of Lebanon" (Ps 92:13).

⁶They kill the widow and alien;
    the orphan they murder.
⁷They say, "The LORD does not see;
    the God of Jacob takes no notice."

III

⁸Understand, you stupid people!
    You fools, when will you be
        wise?
⁹Does the one who shaped the ear
    not hear?
    The one who formed the eye not
        see?
¹⁰Does the one who guides nations
    not rebuke?
    The one who teaches man not
        have knowledge?

¹¹The LORD knows the plans of man;
    they are like a fleeting breath.

IV

¹²Blessed the one whom you guide,
    LORD,
    whom you teach by your
        instruction,
¹³To give rest from evil days,
    while a pit is being dug for the
        wicked.
¹⁴For the LORD will not forsake his
    people,
    nor abandon his inheritance.
¹⁵Judgment shall again be just,
    and all the upright of heart will
        follow it.

How long will God allow this situation to last? In a patriarchal society, the widow, the orphan, and the resident alien have no male guardian and, consequently, lack a legal sponsor or protector. In the Bible, these three groups represent the most vulnerable in society. Here, oppression of them symbolizes the excessive cruelty of the enemies. Their boast is close to blasphemy; they claim that God does not even care about the fate of God's own people.

8-11 The wicked are chided

The psalmist turns on the wicked. "Brutish" might be a better translation of the Hebrew word than "stupid," for these wicked have acted like beasts toward the helpless as well as like fools before God. How could they think that the creator would bestow gifts on creatures and then not use the divine exemplars of those gifts to benefit these very creatures? Compared with God's wisdom, human plans are vapid.

12-15 Praise of God

Using themes from the wisdom tradition, the psalmist praises God's justice. Those who accept divine guidance and instruction will be blessed, while the wicked who refuse to heed God's directives will suffer misfortune. Contrary to what the foolish and wicked think, God will not abandon God's very own people. Justice will again rule in society.

16-23 Trust is in the Lord

Rhetorical questions set the stage for a confession of trust in God. Who will stand in defense of the psalmist? The Lord will. In fact, if God had not

V

¹⁶Who will rise up for me against
the wicked?
Who will stand up for me
against evildoers?
¹⁷If the LORD were not my help,
I would long have been silent in
the grave.
¹⁸When I say, "My foot is slipping,"
your mercy, LORD, holds me up.
¹⁹When cares increase within me,
your comfort gives me joy.

VI

²⁰Can unjust judges be your allies,
those who create burdens by
decree,
²¹Those who conspire against the
just
and condemn the innocent to
death?
²²No, the LORD is my secure height,
my God, my rock of refuge,

²³Who will turn back their evil upon
them
and destroy them for their
wickedness.
Surely the LORD our God will
destroy them!

A Call to Praise and Obedience

95

I

¹Come, let us sing joyfully to the
LORD;
cry out to the rock of our
salvation.
²Let us come before him with a
song of praise,
joyfully sing out our psalms.
³For the LORD is the great God,
the great king over all gods,
⁴Whose hand holds the depths of
the earth;
who owns the tops of the
mountains.

done so in the past, the psalmist would have been relegated to a life of silence. Though not in the Hebrew version, "in the grave" is added in some
translations because of the association of silence with death (cf. Ps 115:17).
God is addressed directly in this acknowledgment of divine protection (vv.
18-19). The care that God shows is the covenantal steadfast love. Once again
the psalmist employs rhetorical questions. Here they prepare for a declaration of commitment. Will allegiance be entrusted to the unjust? No. Security can only be found in the Lord and, being just, the Lord will destroy
the wicked. Therefore, commitment will be made to the Lord alone.

Psalm 95 (liturgical hymn)

1-7a A summons to praise God

A cry goes out to praise the Lord. The psalm is replete with liturgical
allusions. Besides mention of praise and song, there is an invitation to enter,
presumably, a place of worship, where the devout might bow, kneel, and
worship God. The reason for such praise is the greatness of God as witnessed in the marvels of creation. The entire natural world belongs to God,
the sea and the dry land, from the depths of the earth to the heights of the

◄ ⁵The sea and dry land belong to God,
who made them, formed them
by hand.

II

◄ ⁶Enter, let us bow down in worship;
let us kneel before the LORD
who made us.

◄ ⁷For he is our God,
we are the people he shepherds,
the sheep in his hands.

III

Oh, that today you would hear his
voice:

◄ ⁸Do not harden your hearts as at
Meribah,
as on the day of Massah in the
desert.

◄ ⁹There your ancestors tested me;
they tried me though they had
seen my works.

¹⁰Forty years I loathed that
generation;
I said: "This people's heart goes
astray;
they do not know my ways."

¹¹Therefore I swore in my anger:
"They shall never enter my
rest."

God of the Universe

96

I

¹Sing to the LORD a new song;
sing to the LORD, all the earth.

²Sing to the LORD, bless his name;
proclaim his salvation day after
day.

³Tell his glory among the nations;
among all peoples, his
marvelous deeds.

---

mountains. This great God is the special God of the very people called to
give praise. They are cared for by God as a shepherd tends a well-loved
flock.

7b-11 A warning

The psalm takes on an entirely different character. The people are ad-
monished to listen to God and not follow the path taken by their ancestors
who, despite God's solicitous care of them, revolted in the wilderness and
turned away. God tells of their sin and describes their punishment. In consequence of their disloyalty, they were prevented from entering the land
of promise. Instead, they were forced to sojourn in the wilderness for an
entire generation (forty years). All but a few died there (cf. Deut 1:35-39).
The psalm ends on this negative note.

Psalm 96 (kingship of God)

1-3 An invitation to praise

Three times the psalmist calls out: "Sing to the LORD." This is followed
by two exhortations to proclaim God's wondrous deeds of salvation. These
imperatives are addressed to all the earth, all nations, and all peoples.

II

⁴For great is the LORD and highly to
be praised,
to be feared above all gods.
⁵For the gods of the nations are
idols,
but the LORD made the heavens.
⁶Splendor and power go before him;
power and grandeur are in his
holy place.

III

⁷Give to the LORD, you families of
nations,
give to the LORD glory and
might;
⁸give to the LORD the glory due
his name!
Bring gifts and enter his courts;
⁹bow down to the LORD, splendid
in holiness.

Tremble before him, all the earth;
¹⁰declare among the nations: The
LORD is king.
The world will surely stand fast,
never to be shaken.
He rules the peoples with
fairness.

IV

¹¹Let the heavens be glad and the
earth rejoice;
let the sea and what fills it
resound;
¹²let the plains be joyful and all
that is in them.
Then let all the trees of the forest
rejoice
¹³before the LORD who comes,
who comes to govern the earth,
To govern the world with justice
and the peoples with faithfulness.

4-6 Reasons for praise

The reason for the praise is the superiority of this God over the gods of the other nations. They are powerless to accomplish any good thing. The Lord, on the other hand, created the heavens. The holy place to which the psalmist refers here might be God's heavenly dwelling place. However, it could also connote the temple, since Israel believed that it was an earthly representation of that heavenly dwelling.

7-10 A second call to praise

Once again the nations are invited to give glory to God. Here the temple is clearly the focus of attention. It is to this holy place that gifts will be brought as offerings of devotion. It is here that homage will be paid and worship performed. The cry of divine enthronement goes out from this temple: "The LORD is king." God's rule assures that the earth is steadfast and justice reigns among the people.

11-13 Praise from creation

All of creation is called on to praise God. This includes the heavens and the earth. The sea, which in myths of creation is often the chaotic enemy, is here simply a creation of God. It is the habitat of the water creatures that are also called to praise. The God enthroned in the heavens governs the earth with justice and with the covenant characteristic "faithfulness."

The Divine Ruler of All

97

I

¹The LORD is king; let the earth
  rejoice;
  let the many islands be glad.
²Cloud and darkness surround him;
  justice and right are the
    foundation of his throne.
³Fire goes before him,
  consuming his foes on every side.
⁴His lightening illumines the world;
  the earth sees and trembles.
⁵The mountains melt like wax
  before the LORD,

before the Lord of all the earth.
⁶The heavens proclaim his justice;
  all peoples see his glory.

II

⁷All who serve idols are put to
    shame,
  who glory in worthless things;
  all gods bow down before him.
⁸Zion hears and is glad,
  and the daughters of Judah
    rejoice
  because of your judgments, O
    LORD.
⁹For you, LORD, are the Most High
    over all the earth,
  exalted far above all gods.

Psalm 97 (kingship of God)

1-6 The majesty of the divine king

This enthronement psalm opens with the cry of acclamation: "The LORD is king." The scene is one of great power and majesty. All of creation responds to the approach of the mighty ruler. The description, reminiscent of the theophany at Mount Sinai (cf. Exod 19:16-19), signals the appearance of the great storm deity, who comes with clouds and darkness, fire and lightning. This fury causes the earth to tremble; the scorching heat melts the mountains. The God who is so powerful in the heavens is also the one who executes justice on earth.

7-9 Effects of the divine king's coming

Two different yet related consequences follow the coming of the divine king. The first is an acknowledgment of the worthlessness of idols and the shame that accrues for those who worship them. A second effect can be seen in the judgments of God that cause Zion (Jerusalem) and all the surrounding cities to rejoice. The connection between the two is found in the last verse of this section (v. 9). The Lord's superiority over all other deities is captured in the title "Most High." This divine epitaph is the name of the god worshiped in Salem (Jerusalem) before David conquered the city (cf. Gen 14:18).

10-11 The rewards of righteousness

The psalmist lists some of the rewards enjoyed by those who have chosen the path of righteousness. They are loved by God, protected and rescued

¹⁰You who love the LORD, hate evil,
he protects the souls of the
faithful,
rescues them from the hand of
the wicked.
¹¹Light dawns for the just,
and gladness for the honest of
heart.
¹²Rejoice in the LORD, you just,
and give thanks at the remembrance of his holiness.

The Coming of God

98¹A psalm.

I

Sing a new song to the LORD,
for he has done marvelous
deeds.
His right hand and holy arm
have won the victory.

²The LORD has made his victory
known;
has revealed his triumph in the
sight of the nations,
³He has remembered his mercy and
faithfulness
toward the house of Israel.
All the ends of the earth have seen
the victory of our God.

II

⁴Shout with joy to the LORD, all the
earth;
break into song; sing praise.
⁵Sing praise to the LORD with the
lyre,
with the lyre and melodious
song.
⁶With trumpets and the sound of
the horn
shout with joy to the King, the
LORD.

from harm. They live in light rather than darkness, and they enjoy the happiness that comes from this choice.

12 A final exhortation

The psalm ends on a positive note. The righteous are invited to take delight in God and to continue in their praise.

Psalm 98 (kingship of God)

1-3 Praise to the victorious God

The particular divine victory that calls forth songs of praise is difficult to identify with certitude. "[R]ight hand" and "holy arm" are metaphors for military might. The victory took place on earth, not in heaven, for it was witnessed by the other nations. This witness functions as evidence of God's superiority over all other forces. Allusions to the covenant are present in the mention of God's faithful love and in reference to Israel as the recipient of that special love.

4-6 Liturgical celebration of divine kingship

The extensive description of the musical involvement suggests a liturgical celebration. It was probably at such an event that the kingship of God was celebrated.

III

⁷Let the sea and what fills it
resound,
the world and those who dwell
there.
⁸Let the rivers clap their hands,
the mountains shout with them
for joy,
⁹Before the LORD who comes,
who comes to govern the earth,
To govern the world with justice
and the peoples with fairness.

The Holy King

99

I

¹The LORD is king, the peoples
tremble;
he is enthroned on the cherubim, the earth quakes.

²Great is the LORD in Zion,
exalted above all the peoples.
³Let them praise your great and
awesome name:
Holy is he!

II

⁴O mighty king, lover of justice,
you have established fairness;
you have created just rule in
Jacob.
⁵Exalt the LORD, our God;
bow down before his footstool;
holy is he!

III

⁶Moses and Aaron were among his
priests,
Samuel among those who called
on his name;

7-9 Natural creation joins in the celebration

Forces of nature, which in other cultures were considered minor deities, join in the celebration. These include the sea and rivers, thought by some to be chaotic deities. Here they join with the mountains and the inhabitants of the earth in rejoicing in anticipation of the arrival of the divine king, who will come in justice.

Psalm 99 (kingship of God)

1-3 Praise of the divine king

The psalm opens with the standard cry of praise: "The LORD is king." Though God's primary place of enthronement is the heavens, details in the psalm indicate that the site of divine rule is the temple. It is people who tremble, not celestial beings; the cherubim are probably the guardians of the ark of the covenant (cf. Exod 25:18-22); Zion is a reference to Jerusalem, where the temple was built and where God's name was revered in a special way (cf. 1 Kgs 8:16-29). This praise ends with a declaration of God's holiness.

4-5 The God of justice

The praise of God is interrupted by a declaration addressed directly to God. In it God is acclaimed for being just and exercising this justice in Israel,

they called on the LORD, and he
answered them.
[7]From the pillar of cloud he spoke
to them;
they kept his decrees, the law he
had given them.
[8]O LORD, our God, you answered
them;
you were a forgiving God to
them,
though you punished their
offenses.
[9]Exalt the LORD, our God;
bow down before his holy
mountain;
holy is the LORD, our God.

Processional Hymn

100[1]A psalm of thanksgiving.

Shout joyfully to the LORD, all you
lands;
[2]serve the LORD with gladness;
come before him with joyful song.
[3]Know that the LORD is God,
he made us, we belong to him,
we are his people, the flock he
shepherds.
[4]Enter his gates with thanksgiving,
his courts with praise.
Give thanks to him, bless his name;
[5]good indeed is the LORD,
His mercy endures forever,
his faithfulness lasts through
every generation.

---

referred to as "Jacob." God's footstool is a further reference to the ark. This acclamation also ends with a declaration of God's holiness.

6-9 Ancestors praise God

Moses, Aaron, and Samuel, significant figures in Israel's history, were rewarded for their devotion to God. The pillar of cloud led the people through the wilderness (cf. Exod 13:21). Once again God is addressed directly (v. 8), acknowledging both God's forgiveness and God's justice. The psalm ends with a final call to praise God who is acclaimed as holy.

Psalm 100 (hymn)

1b-2 An invitation to praise

Though the superscription classifies this as a psalm of thanksgiving, it has the features of a hymn: a call to praise followed by the reason to give praise. All the earth is invited to worship the Lord. The site where this will take place is the temple.

3-5 Reasons for praise

The Lord's identity as God and Israel's privilege as God's chosen people are cause for praise. This God is both the creator of the people and the one who cares for them. Love and faithfulness underscore the covenant bond, a bond that will endure from generation to generation.

Norm of Life for Rulers

101 ¹A psalm of David.

I

I sing of mercy and justice;
  to you, Lord, I sing praise.
²I study the the way of integrity;
  when will you come to me?
I act with integrity of heart
  within my household.
³I do not allow into my presence
    anything base.
  I hate wrongdoing;
  I will have no part of it.
⁴May the devious heart keep far
    from me;
  the wicked I will not acknowl-
    edge.
⁵Whoever slanders a neighbor in
    secret
  I will reduce to silence.

Haughty eyes and arrogant hearts
  I cannot endure.

II

⁶I look to the faithful of the land
  to sit at my side.
Whoever follows the way of integrity
  is the one to enter my service.
⁷No one who practices deceit
  can remain within my house.
No one who speaks falsely
  can last in my presence.
⁸Morning after morning I clear all
    the wicked from the land,
  to rid the city of the Lord of all
    doers of evil.

Prayer in Time of Distress

102 ¹The prayer of one afflicted and wasting away whose anguish is poured out before the Lord.

Psalm 101 (royal psalm)

1b-3 The upright king

The king begins with praise of God's covenant love and justice, and then moves immediately into a promise to act righteously. (The Hebrew verb forms are future tense.) These promises probably apply more to the king's manner of ruling than simply to his personal life. Integrity of heart (v. 2) is a distinctive characteristic of the king (cf. 1 Kgs 3:6).

4-8 Righteous citizenry

The king not only pledges himself to principled living, but also promises to require the same righteousness of the people in his realm. This will be particularly true of those who serve in court. Since they execute the directives of the king, they must be trusted to do so with the same integrity with which those directives were initially enacted. The king further pledges to enforce this justice daily and with great severity. Most likely, the city of the Lord is Jerusalem.

Psalm 102 (lament of an individual; penitential)

2-3 A cry for help

The lament (considered one of the penitential psalms; cf. Pss 6, 32, 38, 51, 130, 143) opens with the standard cry for help: Hear me! Don't turn

I
²LORD, hear my prayer;
   let my cry come to you.
³Do not hide your face from me
   in the day of my distress.
Turn your ear to me;
   when I call, answer me quickly.
⁴For my days vanish like smoke;
   my bones burn away as in a
      furnace.
⁵My heart is withered, dried up like
     grass,
   too wasted to eat my food.
⁶From my loud groaning
   I become just skin and bones.
⁷I am like a desert owl,
   like an owl among the ruins.
⁸I lie awake and moan,
   like a lone sparrow on the roof.
⁹All day long my enemies taunt me;

   in their rage, they make my
     name a curse.
¹⁰I eat ashes like bread,
   mingle my drink with tears.
¹¹Because of your furious wrath,
   you lifted me up just to cast me
     down.
¹²My days are like a lengthening
     shadow;
   I wither like the grass.

II
¹³But you, LORD, are enthroned
     forever;
   your renown is for all
     generations.
¹⁴You will again show mercy to
     Zion;
   now is the time for pity;
   the appointed time has come.

---

away. Don't allow me to linger in distress, but come to my aid quickly. The tenor of the prayers implies that God can indeed alleviate the suffering under which the psalmist labors.

4-12 The distress

The psalmist does not identify the exact nature of the affliction. Instead, metaphors are used to characterize it. Smoke signifies the emptiness and worthlessness of days as they pass; fire describes the burning nature of the physical pain; lifeless and useless grass characterizes the body that has withered away and is now skin and bones; finally, the afflicted one experiences isolation, like a solitary bird in the wilderness or alone on a roof. Added to these tribulations is the mockery hurled at the psalmist by enemies. Ashes, along with dust, symbolize human mortality (cf. Gen 18:27; Job 30:19; 42:6). Therefore, to eat ashes means to eat death. The psalmist acknowledges that all of this suffering comes from God. In fact, God is described as being somewhat capricious, for this tortured one was lifted up, only to be cast down again.

13-23 Divine mercy

Mention of divine enthronement implies God's conquest over chaos and consequent dominion over all creation. By appealing to this divine supremacy, the psalmist is acknowledging God's power, most likely hoping that this power will be employed to assuage the psalmist's own suffering.

15Its stones are dear to your servants;
 its dust moves them to pity.
16The nations shall fear your name,
  LORD,
 all the kings of the earth, your
  glory,
17Once the LORD has rebuilt Zion
 and appeared in glory,
18Heeding the plea of the lowly,
 not scorning their prayer.
19Let this be written for the next
  generation,
 for a people not yet born,
 that they may praise the LORD:
20"The LORD looked down from the
  holy heights,
 viewed the earth from heaven,
21To attend to the groaning of the
  prisoners,
 to release those doomed to die."

22Then the LORD's name will be
  declared on Zion,
 his praise in Jerusalem,
23When peoples and kingdoms
  gather
 to serve the LORD.

III

24He has shattered my strength in
  mid-course,
 has cut short my days.
25I plead, O my God,
 do not take me in the midst of
  my days.
 Your years last through all
  generations.
26Of old you laid the earth's
  foundations;
 the heavens are the work of
  your hands.

  Attention is directed to the misfortune suffered by Zion, the city of Jerusalem. Mention of its rebuilding indicates that the city has been destroyed, a factor that helps to classify the psalm as exilic or postexilic. The reconstruction of the city, a demonstration of divine compassion and power, will garner praise for the Lord from the other nations. It also instills hope for those who, like the psalmist, are in agony and who turn to God for escape. Just as God will show mercy to Zion (v. 14), so God will hear the cries of the lowly (v. 18) and those who are imprisoned (v. 21). The psalmist appeals to such divine compassion, hoping to be the beneficiary of it as well.

  Another approach is used to win divine assistance. The psalmist suggests that if a report of God's deliverance is preserved for the instruction of the generations to come, they will know that the God enthroned above has compassion on those on earth who are struck down by affliction. Such a report will redound to God's glory, and praise of God's goodness will resound in the restored city of Jerusalem. More than this, other nations and peoples will gather to worship this merciful God.

24-29 A plea for deliverance

  The psalmist extols God's graciousness, perhaps hoping that this acclamation will soften God toward the psalmist's own suffering. Now the psalmist returns to lament. In order that God be persuaded to lift the burden

27They perish, but you remain;
   they all wear out like a garment;
Like clothing you change them and
   they are changed,
   28but you are the same, your
   years have no end.
29May the children of your servants
   live on;
   may their descendants live in
   your presence.

Praise of Divine Goodness

103 1Of David.

I

Bless the LORD, my soul;
   all my being, bless his holy name!
2Bless the LORD, my soul;
   and do not forget all his gifts,

3Who pardons all your sins,
   and heals all your ills,
4Who redeems your life from the pit,
   and crowns you with mercy and
   compassion,
5Who fills your days with good
   things,
   so your youth is renewed like
   the eagle's.

II

6The LORD does righteous deeds,
   brings justice to all the
   oppressed.
7He made known his ways to
   Moses,
   to the Israelites his deeds.
8Merciful and gracious is the LORD,
   slow to anger, abounding in
   mercy.

---

of suffering, appeal is made to two other divine characteristics—God's everlasting nature and unwavering stability. God endures through generation upon generation; the psalmist simply asks to be granted a full complement of years and not be cut off in midlife. In addition to being steadfast, God has established the earth on a firm foundation. But even if the heavens and the earth crumble, God remains; the psalmist asks for some kind of endurance to live on through the future generations. The prayer that began with lament, moved to praise and back to lament, now closes with a request for continuity.

Psalm 103 (hymn)

1-5 An invitation to praise

The same invitation to bless or praise the Lord both opens and closes this psalm, thus acting as a kind of frame enveloping the sentiments expressed. The Hebrew word translated "soul" is actually the "life force" that sustains the entire individual. Thus the call to bless is issued to the most vibrant aspect of the person. Several reasons to praise God are given. Of the gifts bestowed on the psalmist, the most significant are divine love and compassion. Characteristics of God's covenantal commitment, these gifts are probably the reason and source of all other blessings. The eagle was a symbol of rejuvenation and strength (cf. Isa 40:31).

⁹He will not always accuse,
   and nurses no lasting anger;
¹⁰He has not dealt with us as our
      sins merit,
   nor requited us as our wrongs
      deserve.

III

¹¹For as the heavens tower over the
      earth,
   so his mercy towers over those
      who fear him.
¹²As far as the east is from the west,
   so far has he removed our sins
      from us.
¹³As a father has compassion on his
      children,
   so the LORD has compassion on
      those who fear him.

¹⁴For he knows how we are formed,
   remembers that we are dust.
¹⁵As for man, his days are like the
      grass;
   he blossoms like a flower in the
      field.
¹⁶A wind sweeps over it and it is
      gone;
   its place knows it no more.
¹⁷But the LORD's mercy is from age
      to age,
   toward those who fear him.
His salvation is for the children's
      children
¹⁸of those who keep his
      covenant,
   and remember to carry out his
      precepts.

6-18 God's graciousness

The goodness of God is extolled, particularly God's mercy toward Israel, despite its continued disloyalty. First, God's care of the oppressed is acclaimed. This was most evident in the events surrounding the exodus from Egyptian bondage. The psalmist then expounds on God's merciful nature. "Merciful and gracious is the LORD, / slow to anger, abounding in mercy" (v. 8), the divine characterization proclaimed by God after the people had forged a golden calf for themselves in the wilderness (cf. Exod 34:6), became a standard way of describing God's mercy toward sinners (cf. Num 14:18; Neh 9:17; Ps 86:15). The extent of God's steadfast love is compared to the boundless expanse between the heavens and earth; God's willingness to forgive is compared to the vast distance between east and west, as well as the compassion of a human father for his children. Each example highlights a feature that cannot be calculated. In like manner, God's graciousness to those who have been disloyal is immeasurable.

The reason for God's compassion is humanity's fundamental frailty. Human beings are made of worthless dust; they live a very short time, and then they disappear like insubstantial vegetation. Once again a comparison is made. Though human beings are short-lived, God's steadfast love lasts forever. The blessings of the covenant continue through the ages from one generation to the next, to those who are faithful to their own covenant commitment.

IV

¹⁹The LORD has set his throne in
heaven;
his dominion extends over all.
²⁰Bless the LORD, all you his angels,
mighty in strength, acting at his
behest,
obedient to his command.
²¹Bless the LORD, all you his hosts,
his ministers who carry out his
will.
²²Bless the LORD, all his creatures,
everywhere in his domain.
Bless the LORD, my soul!

Praise of God the Creator

◄ 104

I

¹Bless the LORD, my soul!
LORD, my God, you are great
indeed!

You are clothed with majesty and
splendor,
²robed in light as with a cloak.
You spread out the heavens like a
tent;
³setting the beams of your
chambers upon the
waters.
You make the clouds your chariot;
traveling on the wings of the
wind.
⁴You make the winds your
messengers;
flaming fire, your ministers.

II

⁵You fixed the earth on its
foundation,
so it can never be shaken.
⁶The deeps covered it like a garment;
above the mountains stood the
waters.

19-22 Praise of the divine king

Celestial beings are invited to praise God who is enthroned in the heavens. The angels are divine messengers, and the hosts are the heavenly armies. They all serve God faithfully and are here called on to praise or bless the Lord. Finally, everything that God created is called to join the chorus of praise. The psalm ends as it began: "Bless the LORD, my soul!"

Psalm 104 (hymn)

1-4 The God of heaven

Commentators have long recognized the similarities between this hymn and various other ancient Near Eastern songs of praise, particularly the Egyptian "Hymn to Aton." While literary comparison can certainly be made, the major difference is theological. The Egyptian poem celebrates the divinized sun disk, while Israel praises its God as the sole creator.

Like Psalm 103, this psalm opens and closes with the same summons to bless or praise the Lord, but then it moves immediately to acclamations directed to God. In them, God is characterized as the triumphant cosmic warrior who now rules in the heavens as the mighty storm deity. God is clothed in the majesty and glory of the heavens, is housed in a palace that

71

⁷At your rebuke they took flight;
  at the sound of your thunder
    they fled.
⁸They rushed up the mountains,
    down the valleys
  to the place you had fixed for
    them.
⁹You set a limit they cannot pass;
  never again will they cover the
    earth.

III

¹⁰You made springs flow in wadies
  that wind among the mountains.
¹¹They give drink to every beast of
    the field;
  here wild asses quench their
    thirst.
¹²Beside them the birds of heaven
    nest;
  among the branches they sing.
¹³You water the mountains from
  your chambers;

from the fruit of your labor the
    earth abounds.
¹⁴You make the grass grow for the
    cattle
  and plants for people's work
  to bring forth food from the
    earth,
¹⁵wine to gladden their hearts,
  oil to make their faces shine,
  and bread to sustain the human
    heart.
¹⁶The trees of the Lᴏʀᴅ drink their
    fill,
  the cedars of Lebanon, which
    you planted.
¹⁷There the birds build their nests;
  the stork in the junipers, its
    home.
¹⁸The high mountains are for wild
    goats;
  the rocky cliffs, a refuge for
    badgers.

is erected over the defeated waters of chaos, and, like the sun, God travels across the heavens with the clouds and wind as celestial attendants. The flaming fire that accompanies God is probably the lightning.

5-13 Waters of the earth

The once chaotic waters have been tamed and are now an ordered part of the world. The earth was established on them, and boundaries were set so that these waters would not endanger it. God's authority over the waters is evident. They heed God's word, assume the place that God assigns them, and remain within the limits that God set. Once secured, they serve to water the land and quench the thirst of earth's wild animals. The waters that once threatened life now support it. All of this is accomplished by the mighty God who rules from the divine throne established in the heavens. God's distance does not suggest disinterest. Rather, it is evidence of God's supremacy over all.

14-23 God's care of the earth

The description of the earth depicts a peaceful and flourishing paradise. There is food for the animals and bread and wine for human beings. Oil for anointing suggests a level of economic prosperity. Bread, wine, and oil

IV

¹⁹You made the moon to mark the
    seasons,
  the sun that knows the hour of
    its setting.
²⁰You bring darkness and night
    falls,
  then all the animals of the forest
    wander about.
²¹Young lions roar for prey;
  they seek their food from God.
²²When the sun rises, they steal
    away
  and settle down in their dens.
²³People go out to their work,
  to their labor till evening falls.

V

²⁴How varied are your works,
  Lord!

In wisdom you have made them
    all;
  the earth is full of your creatures.
²⁵There is the sea, great and wide!
  It teems with countless beings,
  living things both large and
    small.
²⁶There ships ply their course
  and Leviathan, whom you
    formed to play with.

VI

²⁷All of these look to you
  to give them food in due time.
²⁸When you give it to them, they
    gather;
  when you open your hand, they
    are well filled.
²⁹When you hide your face, they
    panic.

---

are not only fruits of the earth and staples of life, but also products of a society engaged in agriculture and viticulture. Cattle and beasts of burden are domesticated animals implying some form of animal husbandry. The scene depicted is one of order, fulfillment, and stability.

There is also order and satiety outside the realm of human habitation. Trees thrive, as do the animals dependent on them. Topography that is inhospitable toward humans is ideal for certain animals. There they find not only safety but enough food and water to survive and flourish. The orderly movements of the heavens also serve the needs of earth's creatures. The sun and the moon, celestial bodies that were considered divine in other cultures, were demythologized by ancient Israel and now simply mark the seasons and the times of day. Even the regularity of night and day serves the needs of earth's animals. Many of them seek food under the cover of darkness, while human beings thrive in the light of day. Each follows the nature determined by the creator who oversees their activities and provides for their needs.

24-30 Divine providence

The psalmist marvels at the great variety of life-forms found in creation. Not only is this assortment vast and varied, but it also exhibits a kind of interdependence. All the different aspects of creation fit together and work together. This order in the midst of complexity testifies to the divine wisdom

Take away their breath, they
perish
and return to the dust.
³⁰Send forth your spirit, they are
created
and you renew the face of the
earth.

VII

³¹May the glory of the Lord endure
forever;
may the Lord be glad in his
works!
³²Who looks at the earth and it
trembles,
touches the mountains and they
smoke!
³³I will sing to the Lord all my life;
I will sing praise to my God
while I live.

³⁴May my meditation be pleasing to
him;
I will rejoice in the Lord.
³⁵May sinners vanish from the
earth,
and the wicked be no more.
Bless the Lord, my soul!
Hallelujah!

God's Fidelity to the Promise

105

I

¹Give thanks to the Lord, invoke
his name;
make known among the peoples
his deeds!
²Sing praise to him, play music;
proclaim all his wondrous
deeds!

---

that brought it into being in the first place. The sea, once the unruly waters of chaos, is now the home of living creatures. These waters are reliable enough for ships to sail across them. Leviathan, once the monster that characterized chaotic waters (cf. Ps 74:14; Isa 27:1; Job 3:8; 40:25), is now one water animal among many that frolic in the sea. All the creatures of the land and of the sea are dependent on God for sustenance. Their very lives are in God's hands, and they live at the pleasure of the creator. Mention of dust recalls the early account of creation (cf. Gen 2:7, 19) and points to their vulnerability.

31-35 Prayer wishes

The psalm ends with several prayer wishes. The first is for the perpetual endurance of God's glory. This glory is seen in the power that God exercises over creation. The psalmist prays that these very prayers be pleasing to God and, finally, that sinners be punished. To the repetition of the opening summons to bless God is added a second acclamation: "Hallelujah!" Praise (*hallel*) the Lord (*jah*).

Psalm 105 (historical recital)

1-6 A call to give thanks

This historical recital opens with a series of imperatives: "Give thanks . . . / Sing praise . . . play music; / proclaim . . . / Glory . . . / rejoice

³Glory in his holy name;
    let hearts that seek the LORD
      rejoice!
⁴Seek out the LORD and his might;
    constantly seek his face.
⁵Recall the wondrous deeds he has
    done,
    his wonders and words of
      judgment,
⁶You descendants of Abraham his
    servant,
    offspring of Jacob the chosen
      one!

II

⁷He the LORD, is our God
    whose judgments reach through
    all the earth.
⁸He remembers forever his covenant,

the word he commanded for a
    thousand generations,
⁹Which he made with Abraham,
    and swore to Isaac,
¹⁰And ratified in a statute for Jacob,
    an everlasting covenant for Israel:
¹¹"To you I give the land of Canaan,
    your own allotted inheritance."

III

¹²When they were few in number,
    a handful, and strangers there,
¹³Wandering from nation to nation,
    from one kingdom to another
      people,
¹⁴He let no one oppress them;
    for their sake he rebuked kings:
¹⁵"Do not touch my anointed ones,
    to my prophets do no harm."

. . . Seek out . . . / seek." Each in its own way is a summons to extol the greatness of God. While praise can be lifted to God at any time and in any circumstance, mention of playing music suggests a cultic situation. The last imperative, "Recall," explains why such a determined summons is issued. The psalm is addressed to the people of Israel, the descendants of Abraham. They are told to call to mind the wondrous deeds that God accomplished on their behalf.

7-15 The ancestors

Israel begins its story with an account of the promises made to the ancestors concerning numerous descendants and a land of their own (cf. Gen 15:2-18). Though ruler of all the earth, the Lord chose this particular people with whom to enter into covenant. Made first through Abraham, then renewed through Isaac and later through Jacob, this pact was meant to last forever (cf. Gen 17:7). Israel's subsequent history was an unfolding of the fulfillment of these covenant promises. Though in the beginning they were a wandering people (one of their earliest creedal statements identifies Abraham as "a refugee Aramean" [cf. Deut 26:5]), they were always under God's protection. The hand of a much later editor, one who was well acquainted with the monarchy, can be seen in the mention of the prophets and an "anointed." Prophets did not appear until several centuries later, and "anointed" refers to the king, the head of a form of government Israel would adopt centuries after the time of the ancestors.

IV

¹⁶Then he called down a famine on
the land,
destroyed the grain that
sustained them.
¹⁷He had sent a man ahead of them,
Joseph, sold as a slave.
¹⁸They shackled his feet with chains;
collared his neck in iron,
¹⁹Till his prediction came to pass,
and the word of the LORD
proved him true.
²⁰The king sent and released him;
the ruler of peoples set him free.
²¹He made him lord over his
household,
ruler over all his possessions,
²²To instruct his princes as he
desired,
to teach his elders wisdom.

V

²³Then Israel entered Egypt;
Jacob sojourned in the land of
Ham.
²⁴God greatly increased his people,
made them more numerous
than their foes.

²⁵He turned their hearts to hate his
people,
to treat his servants deceitfully.
²⁶He sent his servant Moses,
and Aaron whom he had chosen.
²⁷They worked his signs in Egypt
and wonders in the land of Ham.
²⁸He sent darkness and it grew
dark,
but they rebelled against his
word.
²⁹He turned their waters into blood
and killed their fish.
³⁰Their land swarmed with frogs,
even the chambers of their
kings.
³¹He spoke and there came swarms
of flies,
gnats through all their country.
³²For rain he gave them hail,
flashes of lightning throughout
their land.
³³He struck down their vines and
fig trees,
shattered the trees of their
country.
³⁴He spoke and the locusts came,
grasshoppers without number.

16-22 Israel in Egypt

The story of Israel's ordeal in Egypt begins with the Joseph narrative
(cf. Gen 37–47). This account contains several important aspects of Israelite
faith. Besides explaining the arrival in Egypt of the ancestors of Israel, it
underscores God's special care of them in a foreign land. The rise of one
Israelite (Joseph) within the ranks of the Egyptian government demonstrates
the superior nature of the entire people. Joseph surpassed the Egyptian
sages and magicians with his wisdom, proving that the tradition of Israel
outstripped that of Egypt. The exploits of Joseph gave the nation a reason
to be proud of its heritage.

23-38 Bondage and deliverance

According to both the psalm and the account of Israel's oppression in
Egypt (cf. Exod 1:7), Israel's swell in population contributed toward Egypt's
resentment and the consequent hardships forced upon Israel. Ham was one
of the sons of Noah. The land that bore his name included Egypt (cf. Gen

³⁵They devoured every plant in the
land;
they devoured the crops of their
fields.
³⁶He struck down every firstborn in
the land,
the first fruits of all their vigor.
³⁷He brought his people out,
laden with silver and gold;
no one among the tribes stumbled.
³⁸Egypt rejoiced when they left,
for fear had seized them.

VI

³⁹He spread a cloud out as a cover,
and made a fire to light up the
night.
⁴⁰They asked and he brought them
quail;
with bread from heaven he filled
them.

⁴¹He split the rock and water
gushed forth;
it flowed through the desert like
a river.
⁴²For he remembered his sacred
promise
to Abraham his servant.
⁴³He brought his people out with joy,
his chosen ones with shouts of
triumph.
⁴⁴He gave them the lands of the
nations,
they took possession of the
wealth of the peoples,
⁴⁵That they might keep his statutes
and observe his teachings.
Hallelujah!

Israel's Confession of Sin

106 ¹Hallelujah!

10:6). The land of Ham became a synonym for that country. The effects of the signs and wonders wrought by Moses and Aaron were both positive and negative. They were miracles for the Israelites, but plagues for the Egyptians (cf. Exod 7–11). Regardless of their degree of historical accuracy, these signs and wonders proclaim two major interrelated theological truths: a) The God of Israel has the power to perform marvelous works even in Egypt; b) The God of Israel is actually more powerful than the gods of Egypt.

39-45 Guidance to the land

Escape from Egypt was not enough. The people would have been perpetual wanderers had God not led them into the land promised to their ancestors. The trek from Sinai to Canaan was marked by miracle after miracle. This historical recital recounts only the graciousness of God, not the infidelity of the people, because it is a hymn of praise. (Ps 106 provides another view of the events of history). The psalm closes with the joyful acclamation "Hallelujah!" Praise (*hallel*) the Lord (*jah*).

Psalm 106 (historical recital)

1-3 A call to give thanks

Psalms 105 and 106 could be considered a pair. Both begin with a summons to give thanks to the Lord, both end with the joyful cry "Hallelujah,"

A

Give thanks to the Lord, who is
    good,
    whose mercy endures forever.
²Who can recount the mighty deeds
    of the Lord,
    proclaim in full God's praise?
³Blessed those who do what is
    right,
    whose deeds are always just.
⁴Remember me, Lord, as you favor
    your people;
    come to me with your saving
    help,
⁵That I may see the prosperity of
    your chosen ones,
    rejoice in the joy of your people,
    and glory with your heritage.

B

⁶We have sinned like our ancestors;
    we have done wrong and are
    guilty.

I

⁷Our ancestors in Egypt
    did not attend to your wonders.
They did not remember your
    manifold mercy;
    they defied the Most High at the
    Red Sea.
⁸Yet he saved them for his name's
    sake
    to make his power known.
⁹He roared at the Red Sea and it
    dried up.
He led them through the deep
    as through a desert.
¹⁰He rescued them from hostile
    hands,
    freed them from the power of
    the enemy.
¹¹The waters covered their
    oppressors;
    not one of them survived.
¹²Then they believed his words
    and sang his praise.

---

and both recount events from Israel's history. However, the psalms provide two very different views of this history. All the events recorded in the first psalm describe the marvelous deeds that God accomplished on Israel's behalf, while those in the second recount the infidelity of the people even in the face of God's goodness. This psalm begins and ends with the joyful acclamation "Hallelujah!" This is followed by the summons to thank God for all of the goodness that God has shown, particularly for God's steadfast covenant love. Righteous living is affirmed by means of a beatitude.

4-5 A fervent prayer

The psalmist prays to be among those who are blessed by God. The reference is to the chosen people who have been delivered by God and granted a share in the land of promise ("your heritage").

6-12 Deliverance from Egypt

This section opens with an admission of guilt. Though the psalm recounts the sins of the ancestors, the psalmist includes the present generation in the company of those who have done wrong: "We have sinned . . . / we have done wrong." The events of escape from Egypt (cf. Exod 14) are condensed into a description of divine victory over waters, reminiscent of

II

[13]But they soon forgot all he had
done;
  they had no patience for his
  plan.
[14]In the desert they gave in to their
cravings,
  tempted God in the wasteland.
[15]So he gave them what they asked
  and sent a wasting disease
  against them.

III

[16]In the camp they challenged Moses
  and Aaron, the holy one of the
  LORD.
[17]The earth opened and swallowed
Dathan,

it closed on the followers of
Abiram.
[18]Against their company the fire
blazed;
  flames consumed the wicked.

IV

[19]At Horeb they fashioned a calf,
  worshiped a metal statue.
[20]They exchanged their glory
  for the image of a grass-eating
  bull.
[21]They forgot the God who had
saved them,
  who had done great deeds in
  Egypt,
[22]Amazing deeds in the land of Ham,
  fearsome deeds at the Red Sea.

---

the ancient Near Eastern story of creation. Just as God had cut through the waters of primordial chaos and ordered the cosmic world, so God separated the waters that represent political oppression for the people and transformed them into a new nation. The primary purpose of this particular historical recital might be seen in verses 7 and 8; the people were oblivious of the magnanimous goodness of God, and yet God saved them out of even greater goodness. On the other side of freedom, they sang songs of praise. However, the remainder of the psalm will show that this piety was short-lived.

13-18 Infidelity in the wilderness

The alternation between blessing and transgression continues in the wilderness (cf. Num 16). Each demonstration of divine providence is met with an act of rebellion. Despite this, when the people grumbled and made demands on God, God responded by granting their request. Eventually, however, their infidelity was requited; they were punished for their sinfulness. When they were disgruntled, they turned against their leaders and were punished for this as well. They did not learn from their misfortune, but continued their rebellious behavior.

19-23 The sin of idolatry

Perhaps their most ignominious betrayal occurred at the foot of the very mountain from which God delivered the law (cf. Exod 32:1-14). There they fashioned an idol for themselves, choosing to worship lifeless metal rather

²³He would have decreed their
destruction,
had not Moses, his chosen one,
Withstood him in the breach
to turn back his destroying
anger.

V

²⁴Next they despised the beautiful
land;
they did not believe the
promise.
²⁵In their tents they complained;
they did not heed the voice of
the LORD.
²⁶So with raised hand he swore
he would destroy them in the
desert,
²⁷And scatter their descendants
among the nations,
disperse them in foreign lands.

VI

²⁸They joined in the rites of Baal of
Peor,
ate food sacrificed to the dead.
²⁹They provoked him by their
actions,
and a plague broke out among
them.
³⁰Then Phinehas rose to intervene,
and the plague was brought to a
halt.
³¹This was counted for him as a
righteous deed
for all generations to come.

VII

³²At the waters of Meribah they
angered God,
and Moses suffered because of
them.
³³They so embittered his spirit
that rash words crossed his lips.

than the living God who had delivered them from bondage, provided for their needs in the wilderness, and protected them from harm. Moses, the very man they had turned against, intervened on their behalf and staved off the destructive hand of God. In each case recalled, despite their treacherous behavior, God's wrath is assuaged and the people are given another chance.

24-27 The people's distrust

The people left Egypt in order to settle in a land they could call their own. Their initial reluctance to enter that land, because of the fearsome reports about it that were brought by scouts (cf. Num 14:1-25), illustrated their lack of trust in God. The only explanation for their mistrust of the very God who showed such power in Egypt and such kindness and patience during their sojourn in the wilderness is their hardness of heart. Since they doubted the desirability of the land that God had chosen for them, God ordained that they would not live to enter it. Since the descendants of this generation did indeed enter the land, mention of the dispersal of descendants is probably a reference to a later generation that experienced the exile.

28-31 A second sin of idolatry

Peor, the site where the people of God sinned by worshiping the Canaanite storm god Baal, was located in Moab on the eastern shore of the

VIII

34They did not destroy the peoples
   as the LORD had commanded
      them,
35But mingled with the nations
   and imitated their ways.
36They served their idols
   and were ensnared by them.
37They sacrificed to demons
   their own sons and daughters,
38Shedding innocent blood,
   the blood of their own sons and
      daughters,
Whom they sacrificed to the idols
   of Canaan,
   desecrating the land with blood-
      shed.
39They defiled themselves by their
   actions,
became adulterers by their
   conduct.
40So the LORD grew angry with his
   people,
   abhorred his own heritage.
41He handed them over to the
   nations,
   and their adversaries ruled over
      them.
42Their enemies oppressed them,
   kept them under subjection.
43Many times did he rescue them,
   but they kept rebelling and
      scheming
   and were brought low by their
      own guilt.
44Still God had regard for their
   affliction
   when he heard their wailing.

Jordan River. This betrayal was associated with sexual impropriety with some foreign women. The punishment of the people was shortened by the retributive zeal of the priest Phineas (cf. Num 25:1-13). Once again the people sinned and were punished, but then God relented.

32-33 The sin of Moses

It was because of the incident at Meribah that Moses was prevented from entering the land of promise (cf. Num 20:2-13). The people's demand for water so angered him that he deviated from the trust in God that should have motivated him and he spoke rash words to them.

34-39 Infidelity in the land of promise

The people continued their sinful ways even after having been brought miraculously into the land of promise. The violence they were directed to execute on the original inhabitants of Canaan often offends the sensitivities of contemporary readers, because it appears that God directed it. Without defending the slaughter, it is important to understand why the people would think that this is what God would want. Though Israel was the nation moving into the territory of another people, as a nation it was still vulnerable. Realizing how susceptible they were to the religious practices of others, the Israelites believed that the best way to prevent such betrayal was to eliminate the other people. They did in fact succumb to idolatrous worship, even practicing child sacrifice and engaging in sex as part of the fertility cults.

⁴⁵For their sake he remembered his
    covenant
and relented in his abundant
    mercy,
⁴⁶Winning for them compassion
    from all who held them captive.

C

⁴⁷Save us, LORD, our God;
    gather us from among the nations
That we may give thanks to your
    holy name

and glory in praising you.
⁴⁸Blessed be the LORD, the God of
    Israel,
from everlasting to everlasting!
Let all the people say, Amen!
Hallelujah!

Fifth Book—Psalms 107–150

God the Savior of Those in Distress

107 ¹"Give thanks to the LORD for
    he is good,

40-46 God's response to sin

God's response to Israel's sinfulness in the land was the same as it had been when the people were in the wilderness. God's anger flared, the people endured chastisement for their transgressions, and eventually God relented. Once they were settled in the land, the punishment took the form of defeat at the hands of their enemies. The ultimate punishment was the defeat by the Babylonians and exile in the land of their conquerors. This was probably the captivity referred to here (v. 46). Even in that situation, God's steadfast covenant love for the people prevailed. The hearts of the captors were softened and they were kindly disposed toward God's people. The stage was set for their release.

47 A prayer for deliverance

The prayer to be gathered from among the nations suggests the dispersal of the people at the time of the exile. Their release, reunion, and return to their land will prompt them to thank and praise God continually.

48 Final doxology

The final prayer of praise is the conclusion of the entire fourth book of the Psalter. It contains many of the same sentiments found in the conclusions of the other books (cf. Pss 41:14; 72:18-20; 89:53). Unlike the others, this book ends as the psalm began, with the traditional acclamation of praise: "Hallelujah!" Praise (*hallel*) the Lord (*jah*).

BOOK FIVE: PSALMS 107–150

Psalm 107 (prayer of confidence of an individual)

1-3 A call to give thanks

The psalmist calls the people to give thanks to God. Mention of God's love suggests a covenant relationship. Identifying the people as those who

his mercy endures forever!"
²Let that be the prayer of the LORD's
    redeemed,
    those redeemed from the hand
        of the foe,
³Those gathered from foreign lands,
    from east and west, from north
        and south.

I

⁴Some had lost their way in a barren
    desert;
    found no path toward a city to
        live in.
⁵They were hungry and thirsty;
    their life was ebbing away.

⁶In their distress they cried to the
    LORD,
    who rescued them in their peril,
⁷Guided them by a direct path
    so they reached a city to live in.
⁸Let them thank the LORD for his
    mercy,
    such wondrous deeds for the
        children of Adam.
⁹For he satisfied the thirsty,
    filled the hungry with good
        things.

II

¹⁰Some lived in darkness and gloom,
    imprisoned in misery and chains.

have been redeemed and gathered from all directions suggests the period after the exile. The people's redemption and return to the land of promise would be ample reason for giving thanks.

4-9 Hardships en route

The hardships described in this section could refer either to the trials endured as the people traveled from their place of exile in Babylon back to their home in Israel, or to an earlier time when their ancestors moved from bondage in Egypt to the land promised by God. Most likely, this tradition of hardship was originally associated with the earlier period and then employed poetically in describing the latter one. Whichever period is the focus of this description, the point made is the same, namely, the people cried to God in their need, and God responded.

This is the first of four descriptions of suffering endured by some of the population. In each case the suffering is identified. This first description is followed by a report that serves almost as a refrain: "In their distress they cried to the LORD, / who rescued them in their peril" (vv. 6, 13, 19, 28). Finally, the people are called to give thanks: "Let them thank the LORD for his mercy [the word for covenant love], / such wondrous deeds for the children of Adam" (vv. 8, 15, 21, 31). Here, the people remember that they were wandering with no direction, and God guided them to safety.

10-16 Hardships of prison

The descriptions in these sections do not appear to follow any chronological order. The previous verses described the hardships with which the people were afflicted while they were on their return from exile. These

[11]Because they rebelled against
    God's word,
  and scorned the counsel of the
    Most High,
[12]He humbled their hearts through
    hardship;
  they stumbled with no one to
    help.
[13]In their distress they cried to the
    LORD,
  who saved them in their peril;
[14]He brought them forth from dark-
    ness and the shadow of
    death
  and broke their chains asunder.
[15]Let them thank the LORD for his
    mercy,
  such wondrous deeds for the
    children of Adam.
[16]For he broke down the gates of
    bronze
  and snapped the bars of iron.

III

[17]Some fell sick from their wicked
    ways,
  afflicted because of their sins.
[18]They loathed all manner of food;
  they were at the gates of death.
[19]In their distress they cried to the
    LORD,
  who saved them in their peril,
[20]Sent forth his word to heal them,
  and snatched them from the
    grave.
[21]Let them thank the LORD for his
    mercy,
  such wondrous deeds for the
    children of Adam.
[22]Let them offer a sacrifice in
    thanks,
  recount his works with shouts
    of joy.

---

verses revert to a time of imprisonment. The hardship may have been se-
vere, but the psalmist maintains that it was justifiable punishment. The
people had violated their covenant agreement, rejected divine counsel, and
rebelled against God. Initially, they were bereft of help, but eventually God
relented and came to their rescue, releasing them from their bondage. Here
too they cried out, were heard, and were subsequently summoned to give
thanks to God.

17-22 Stricken with illness

A third type of suffering is described. Some of the company were
stricken with illness, which was yet another consequence of their sins. Unable to eat, they almost died. However, after they cried for help, God
snatched them from the jaws of death. Besides being called to give thanks,
here the people are exhorted to offer sacrifice as well.

23-32 Deliverance of seafarers

The last descriptive section reports trials at sea. Such experiences would
have been markedly unusual for most of the land-bound early Israelites,
though quite common for those who lived near cities like Tyre and who
made their living through maritime trade (cf. Ezek 27–28). The language

IV

²³Some went off to sea in ships,
plied their trade on the deep
waters.
²⁴They saw the works of the LORD,
the wonders of God in the deep.
²⁵He commanded and roused a
storm wind;
it tossed the waves on high.
²⁶They rose up to the heavens, sank
to the depths;
their hearts trembled at the
danger.
²⁷They reeled, staggered like
drunkards;
their skill was of no avail.
²⁸In their distress they cried to the
LORD,
who brought them out of their
peril;
²⁹He hushed the storm to silence,
the waves of the sea were
stilled.
³⁰They rejoiced that the sea grew
calm,

that God brought them to the
harbor they longed for.
³¹Let them thank the LORD for his
mercy,
such wondrous deeds for the
children of Adam.
³²Let them extol him in the
assembly of the people,
and praise him in the council of
the elders.

V

³³God changed rivers into desert,
springs of water into thirsty
ground,
³⁴Fruitful land into a salty waste,
because of the wickedness of its
people.
³⁵He changed the desert into pools
of water,
arid land into springs of water,
³⁶And settled the hungry there;
they built a city to live in.
³⁷They sowed fields and planted
vineyards,
brought in an abundant harvest.

---

used is highly mythological, which adds a sinister dimension to this description. The sea, the turbulent waters, and the storm winds were all manifestations of the Canaanite storm god. While these forces threatened the lives of sailors, they were no match for the God of Israel whose mere word first provoked their fury and then quelled it. The frightened mariners cried to God; they were heard and finally brought to safe harbor. Once again the people are called on to give thanks to the Lord, to praise God both in the religious assembly of the people and in the council of the ruling elders.

33-43 The providence of God

The preceding sections have been reports of past favors. The present form of verbs used here indicates that this is the way that God acts even now. The once-fertile land of the wicked is turned into a salty, barren wasteland, while the hungry are settled in a land that was once a desert but now yields an abundant harvest. Both the people and their flocks thrive and increase there. This description is reminiscent of the tradition of Israel's

³⁸God blessed them, and they
increased greatly,
and their livestock did not
decrease.
³⁹But he poured out contempt on
princes,
made them wander trackless
wastes,
⁴⁰Where they were diminished and
brought low
through misery and cruel
oppression.
⁴¹While he released the poor man
from affliction,
and increased their families like
flocks.
⁴²The upright saw this and rejoiced;
all wickedness shut its mouth.
⁴³Whoever is wise will take note of
these things,
and ponder the merciful deeds
of the LORD.

Prayer for Victory

108

¹A song; a psalm of David.

I

²My heart is steadfast, God;
my heart is steadfast.
Let me sing and chant praise.
³Awake, lyre and harp!
I will wake the dawn.
⁴I will praise you among the
peoples, LORD;
I will chant your praise among
the nations.
⁵For your mercy is greater than the
heavens;
your faithfulness, to the skies.

II

⁶Appear on high over the heavens,
God;
your glory above all the earth.

---

occupation of the land of promise where God dislodged one people in order to settle another. The reason given for such a reversal of fortune is the sinfulness of one people and the neediness of the other. Such circumstances serve as a lesson for the future.

Psalm 108 (communal lament)

The psalm is a composite, consisting of sections from two earlier psalms: verses 2-6 repeat Psalm 57:8-12; verses 7-14 repeat Psalm 60:8-14.

2-6 The psalmist's devotion

The first part of the psalm is a testimony to the psalmist's piety. Praise of God springs from one who rises at dawn, most likely following a night of prayer. Mention of musical instruments suggests some form of liturgical celebration. The prayer is offered, not privately, but publicly so that it can be witnessed by all. It is rooted in God's own covenant devotion, in divine love and faithfulness that surpass anything earthly. The psalmist requests a manifestation of God originating in the heavens and visible over the entire world.

⁷Help with your right hand and answer us
that your loved ones may escape.
⁸God speaks in his holiness:
"I will exult, I will apportion
Shechem;
the valley of Succoth I will
measure out.
⁹Gilead is mine, mine is Manasseh;
Ephraim is the helmet for my
head,
Judah, my scepter.
¹⁰Moab is my washbowl;
upon Edom I cast my sandal;

I will shout in triumph over
Philistia."
¹¹Who will bring me to the fortified
city?
Who will lead me into Edom?
¹²Was it not you who rejected us,
God?
Do you no longer march with
our armies?
¹³Give us aid against the foe;
worthless is human help.
¹⁴We will triumph with the help of
God,
who will trample down our foes.

---

7 A plea for help

Speaking in the name of the entire community, the psalmist pleads for divine assistance. The right hand is traditionally considered the stronger hand, the one that wields the weapon of defense.

8-10 God speaks

A divine oracle, issued from the sanctuary, calls to mind the promise that Israel will occupy the land. The military success needed to realize this promise functions as grounds for hope of deliverance from present peril. Shechem was situated in northern Israel between Mounts Ebal and Gerizim. The valley of Succoth was just east of the Jordan River. Gilead and Manasseh were regions in Transjordan, while Ephraim, a common name for the northern tribes, and Judah, the name given to the southern tribes, were regions west of the river. All these territories were part of the united kingdom of David. On the other hand, Moab and Edom were independent nations just south of Gilead on the eastern side of the Jordan, and Philistia was a nation west of Judah on the eastern coast of the Mediterranean Sea. The oracle promises that these nations will all come under the control of Israel's God. Their combined borders will constitute the boundaries of the kingdom of Israel.

11-14 Does God hear?

God may be the hero who conquers these territories, but the assaults that Israel suffers indicate that at this point God does not march with Israel's armies. Instead, God seems to have abandoned the people, or at least refused to listen to their pleading. Still, the psalmist is not deterred, but continues to cry to God for relief, convinced that only divine assistance can ensure ultimate triumph.

Prayer of a Person Falsely Accused

109

¹For the leader. A psalm of David.

I

²O God, whom I praise, do not be
silent,
for wicked and treacherous
mouths attack me.
They speak against me with lying
tongues;
³with hateful words they
surround me,
attacking me without cause.
⁴In return for my love they slander
me,
even though I prayed for them.
⁵They repay me evil for good,
hatred for my love.

II

⁶Appoint an evil one over him,
an accuser to stand at his right
hand,
⁷That he may be judged and found
guilty,
that his plea may be in vain.
⁸May his days be few;
may another take his office.
⁹May his children be fatherless,
his wife, a widow.
¹⁰May his children wander and beg,
driven from their hovels.
¹¹May the usurer snare all he owns,
strangers plunder all he earns.
¹²May no one treat him with mercy
or pity his fatherless children.
¹³May his posterity be destroyed,

Psalm 109 (lament of an individual)

1-5 The lament

The psalmist, who is described as the victim of lying enemies, turns to God for help. There is no reason for such ill treatment by others; the psalmist has shown love to and even prayed for the very people who are now acting in such a despicable manner. In this case, kindness is repaid with malice; love is met with hatred.

6-19 The treachery of the enemies

What follows is a very controversial section. The speaker is cursing enemies, calling calamities down on their heads. Many commentators are reluctant to ascribe such sentiments to the psalmist, and so some translations insert words at the beginning of this section (v. 5c) that suggest that it is really the enemies who hurl the imprecations at the psalmist rather than the psalmist speaking with such hatred. While such revision might exonerate the psalmist, it tends to minimize the depths of anger that the psalmist and righteous people sometimes feel in the face of oppression.

Curses are pronounced over various aspects of life. Since justice is necessary in all societies, lying in court is a serious offense and a serious threat to social order. The testimony of the accuser (the Hebrew has *satan*), will result in the innocent defendant suffering the consequences of guilt. The widow and orphaned children of one who meets an untimely death will

their name rooted out in the
next generation.
¹⁴May his fathers' guilt be
mentioned to the LORD;
his mother's sin not rooted out.
¹⁵May their guilt be always before
the LORD,
till their memory is banished
from the earth,
¹⁶For he did not remember to show
mercy,
but hounded the wretched poor
and brought death to the
brokenhearted.
¹⁷He loved cursing; may it come
upon him;
he hated blessing; may none
come to him.

¹⁸May cursing clothe him like a robe;
may it enter his belly like water,
his bones like oil.
¹⁹May it be near as the clothes he
wears,
as the belt always around him.
²⁰May this be the reward for my
accusers from the LORD,
for those speaking evil against
me.

III

²¹But you, LORD, are my Lord,
deal kindly with me for your
name's sake;
in your great mercy rescue me.
²²For I am poor and needy;
my heart is pierced within me.

---

be left with no male protector. If the family goods are confiscated, these poor people will be forced into deplorable destitution. Early Israel did not have a clear understanding of reward or punishment after death. They believed that restitution was frequently exacted in the next generation, children carrying the burden of guilt of their predecessors and suffering the punishment due such sins. The speaker calls this fate down on the stricken individual. The final and perhaps greatest misfortune would be the total eradication of one's name. With no one to do the remembering, it would be as if the person had never even existed. This would be a fate worse than death. The speaker next calls for punishment that fits the crime: the wicked one is accused of loving to curse, so let the curse fall back on the one cursing; since he did not engage in blessing, may he never know blessing. The final curse calls down a curse itself. May it surround this one like a garment; may it enter the deepest regions of his being.

20 Reversal or ratification?

If it was the enemies who were calling down the curses on the psalmist, in this section the psalmist prays that the curses hurled by these enemies fall on them instead. If it was the psalmist pronouncing these imprecations, here he prays that they be ratified by God and enacted against the enemies.

21-31 A plea for divine assistance

Turning to God in supplication, the psalmist appeals to God's faithful commitment to the covenant relationship (vv. 21, 26). The psalmist's

²³Like a lengthening shadow I am
gone,
I am shaken off like the locust.
²⁴My knees totter from fasting;
my flesh has wasted away.
²⁵I have become a mockery to them;
when they see me, they shake
their heads.
²⁶Help me, Lord, my God;
save me in your mercy.
²⁷Make them know this is your hand,
that you, Lord, have done this.
²⁸Though they curse, may you
bless;
arise, shame them, that your
servant may rejoice.
²⁹Clothe my accusers with disgrace;
make them wear their shame
like a mantle.
³⁰I will give fervent thanks to the
Lord;
before a crowd I will praise him.

³¹For he stands at the right hand of
the poor
to save him from those who
pass judgment on him.

God Appoints the King both King and Priest

110 ¹A psalm of David.
The Lord says to my lord:
"Sit at my right hand,
while I make your enemies your
footstool."
²The scepter of your might:
the Lord extends your strong
scepter from Zion.
Have dominion over your enemies!
³Yours is princely power from the
day of your birth.
In holy splendor before the
daystar,
like dew I begot you.

---

miserable condition resembles the end of life as it ebbs away. The suffering is both interior (heart) and physical (tottering knees, wasted flesh). This sufferer's condition prompts mockery from enemies. The psalmist offers a second prayer for help and begs for some sign from God that will let the persecutors know that God is indeed on the psalmist's side. The psalmist asks for reversals: though enemies desire the psalmist's downfall, may God bestow blessing instead. The psalm ends on a note of confidence. God is the protector of the poor, and will stand in their defense.

Psalm 110 (royal psalm)

1-3 Royal enthronement

The first Lord is really YHWH, the personal name of Israel's God; the second lord (*adonai*) probably refers to the king. The enthronement scene is quite striking. It is God who enthrones the king in the ultimate place of honor, at God's right hand. Under the king's feet are his enemies, placed there by God. From Zion, the mountain on which Jerusalem stands, the king rules over all the nations. Traces of ancient Near Eastern royal ideology can be seen in the reference to the father-son relationship between the deity and the human king. The metaphor of the daystar is rich with implications. It may refer to the divine origin of the king's rule, the freshness of its po-

◄ ⁴The LORD has sworn and will not
waver:
"You are a priest forever in the
manner of Melchizedek."
⁵At your right hand is the Lord,
who crushes kings on the day of
his wrath,
⁶Who judges nations, heaps up
corpses,
crushes heads across the wide
earth,
⁷Who drinks from the brook by the
wayside
and thus holds high his head.

Praise of God for Goodness to Israel

111
¹Hallelujah!
I will praise the LORD with all my
heart
in the assembled congregation
of the upright.
²Great are the works of the LORD,
studied by all who delight in
them.
³Majestic and glorious is his work,
his righteousness endures
forever.

---

tential, or the enlightenment brought by this king. The fact that this is a divine oracle gives religious legitimation to the king and his rule.

4 Priestly dignity

A second oracle bestows priestly dignity on the king. The name Melchizedek comes from the Hebrew *melek* (king) and *zedek* (righteous). How the king will function as priest is probably not as important as the connections made between the ruler in Jerusalem and earlier religious traditions (cf. Gen 14:18; Isa 11:1-5).

5-7 Royal success

The scene has changed; it is no longer the place of enthronement, but the battlefield of the world. God, who is here referred to as "Lord," is now at the right hand of the king, acting with force and ensuring victory. It should be noted that the goal of this victory is justice ("judges nations"), not vengeance, and the end of such struggle is honor ("holds high his head").

Psalm 111 (hymn)

The psalm is acrostic, but this characteristic is lost in translation. Though an acrostic structure is a trait of a wisdom psalm, here the content suggests a different classification.

1 Praise of God

The psalm opens with a declaration of praise: *hallel* (praise) *jah* (the Lord). This is followed by a second summons to praise God publicly.

2-9 Reasons for praise

While other psalms describe the wonders of creation as "majesty and splendor" (cf. Ps 104:1), the reference here seems to be to the marvelous

⁴He won renown for his wondrous
deeds;
gracious and merciful is the
LORD.
⁵He gives food to those who fear
him,
he remembers his covenant
forever.
⁶He showed his powerful deeds to
his people,
giving them the inheritance of
the nations.
⁷The works of his hands are true
and just,
reliable all his decrees,
⁸Established forever and ever,

to be observed with truth and
equity.
⁹He sent release to his people,
decreed his covenant forever;
holy and fearsome is his name.
¹⁰The fear of the LORD is the
beginning of wisdom;
prudent are all who practice it.
His praise endures forever.

The Blessings of the Just

112 ¹Hallelujah!
Blessed the man who fears the LORD,
who greatly delights in his
commands.

---

deeds that God performed in redeeming the people of Israel and granting them a land of their own. Besides the explicit mention of covenant (vv. 5, 9), there are other references to elements of the covenant: "gracious and merciful" (v. 4; cf. Exod 34:6), identification of the people as God's people (v. 5). Providing food for the people could be a reference to God's care of them during their sojourn in the wilderness (v. 5; cf. Exod 16:4-36; Num 11:31-34). There is explicit mention of God's gift of the land (v. 6). Decree (v. 7) is a traditional word for law. Finally, mention of deliverance recalls the people's escape from Egypt (v. 9; cf. Exod 14:10-22). All these wondrous deeds prompt the psalmist to call for praise.

10 True wisdom

The psalm ends with *the* classic wisdom adage. Fear of the Lord is really awe in the presence of the almighty God. Anyone with this attitude is on the right path to wisdom. The list of blessings found in this psalm should call forth the kind of awe or "fear of the LORD" that will lead to this wisdom. The psalm ends as it began, with praise of God.

Psalm 112 (wisdom psalm)

This psalm is a companion to Psalm 111. It begins with the same declaration of praise, and it follows the same acrostic structure.

1 Praise and fear of the Lord

The psalm opens with two very distinct literary forms. The first is a declaration of praise: *hallel* (praise) *jah* (the Lord). The second is a beatitude, a

²His descendants shall be mighty in
the land,
a generation of the upright will
be blessed.
³Wealth and riches shall be in his
house;
his righteousness shall endure
forever.
⁴Light shines through the darkness
for the upright;
gracious, compassionate, and
righteous.
⁵It is good for the man gracious in
lending,
who conducts his affairs with
justice.
⁶For he shall never be shaken;
the righteous shall be
remembered forever.
⁷He shall not fear an ill report;
his heart is steadfast, trusting
the LORD.
⁸His heart is tranquil, without fear,
till at last he looks down on his
foes.
⁹Lavishly he gives to the poor;
his righteousness shall endure
forever;
his horn shall be exalted in honor.
¹⁰The wicked sees and is angry;
gnashes his teeth and wastes
away;
the desire of the wicked come to
nothing.

typical wisdom form that states the blessedness of those who choose a particular way of life. Here the blessed ones are those who fear the Lord. Using parallel construction, the psalmist defines fear of the Lord as "delight[] in [God's] commands."

2-9 Blessings that follow fear of the Lord

Various blessings follow this fundamental attitude of mind and heart. These blessings are not limited to one generation, but will flow over into the lives of descendants. In accord with the theory of retribution, those who fear the Lord will be granted wealth; their righteousness will be seen by all and will be remembered. Even if hardship befalls them, they will continue to trust in God. Finally, they do not hoard their good fortune to themselves, but they share it with those less fortunate. The horn is a symbol of strength; the strength of the righteous will be honored. Those who fear the Lord are people of integrity and unselfishness.

10 The envy of the wicked

The good fortune of the righteous will be the envy of the wicked. The wicked will not only be saddened by this but also be forced to endure the failure of their own aspirations.

93

Praise of God's Care for the Poor

◄ 113 ¹Hallelujah!

I

Praise, you servants of the LORD,
praise the name of the LORD.
²Blessed be the name of the LORD
both now and forever.
³From the rising of the sun to its
setting
let the name of the LORD be
praised.

II

⁴High above all nations is the LORD;
above the heavens his glory.
⁵Who is like the LORD our God,
enthroned on high,
⁶looking down on heaven and
earth?
⁷He raises the needy from the dust,
lifts the poor from the ash heap,
⁸Seats them with princes,
the princes of the people,
⁹Gives the childless wife a home,
the joyful mother of children.
Hallelujah!

Psalm 113 (hymn)

1-3 A call to praise

The psalm opens and closes with "Hallelujah!" The call to praise is issued twice in the first verse. Also identified three times in this section is the object of the praise, namely, the name of the Lord. God's servants are called to praise continually, from dawn to dusk.

4-6 God's universal reign

The Lord is said to rule over heaven and all the nations of the earth as well. The reference to God's enthronement on high suggests the honor bestowed on the divine conqueror of primordial chaos. It is from that singular vantage point that the creator rules over all. There, in the highest regions of the heavens, the glory of God is manifested.

7-9 God's care of the needy

God is not only glorious, but gracious toward the needy as well. Some commentators hold that the elevation of the destitute to the company of royalty is really a reference to the rise of David from humble means to the throne of Israel. Childless women suffered discrimination because they failed to make the contribution to society that was expected of them. This psalm praises God for the reversal of the fortunes of the unfortunate.

Psalm 114 (historical recital)

1-2 God's special people

The psalm describes Israel's release from Egypt. Though the name of the ancestor Jacob was changed to Israel (cf. Gen 35:10), both names are

The Lord's Wonders at the Exodus

114 ¹When Israel came forth from Egypt,
　the house of Jacob from an alien people,
²Judah became God's sanctuary,
　Israel, God's domain.
³The sea saw and fled;
　the Jordan turned back.
⁴The mountains skipped like rams;
　the hills, like lambs.
⁵Why was it, sea, that you fled?
　Jordan, that you turned back?
⁶Mountains, that you skipped like rams?
　You hills, like lambs?

⁷Tremble, earth, before the Lord,
　before the God of Jacob,
⁸Who turned the rock into pools of water,
　flint into a flowing spring.

The Greatness of the True God

115

¹Not to us, LORD, not to us
　but to your name give glory
　because of your mercy and faithfulness.
²Why should the nations say,
　"Where is their God?"

---

used in poetry to refer to the nation. The "sanctuary" in Judah is Jerusalem. The entire nation is the special place of divine rule.

3-6 Nature responds to God's deliverance of the people

Victory over the sea, the symbol of primordial chaotic waters, is the ultimate sign of divine sovereign power. Israel's release began with the people going forth from Egypt through the Reed Sea and ended with them crossing the Jordan River into the land of promise. The skipping of the mountains and hills is probably a reference to the trembling of Mount Sinai at the time of the manifestation of God. What must have originally terrified the people is, in the sight of God, mere playfulness.

7-8 A call to revere God

Just as the mountains and hills quaked before God, so the earth or land is called to tremble in God's presence. Divine power had already shown itself on the earth by means of the miracles performed for the people while they sojourned in the wilderness, where water came from the rocks (cf. Num 20:1-11). It was only right to revere the God who performed such wonders.

Psalm 115 (communal prayer of confidence)

Though some ancient manuscripts join Psalms 114 and 115, commentators today recognize the differences between them.

1-2 Glory belongs to the Lord

There appears to be a contradiction in the first two verses of this psalm. In the first verse, the people decline any praise for themselves and direct

◄ ³Our God is in heaven
    and does whatever he wills.

II

◄ ⁴Their idols are silver and gold,
    the work of human hands.
◄ ⁵They have mouths but do not
      speak,
    eyes but do not see.
  ⁶They have ears but do not hear,
    noses but do not smell.
  ⁷They have hands but do not feel,
    feet but do not walk;
    they produce no sound from
      their throats.
◄ ⁸Their makers will be like them,

and anyone who trusts in them.

III

⁹The house of Israel trusts in the
    LORD,
    who is their help and shield.
¹⁰The house of Aaron trusts in the
    LORD,
    who is their help and shield.
¹¹Those who fear the LORD trust in
    the LORD,
    who is their help and shield.
¹²The LORD remembers us and will
    bless us,
    will bless the house of Israel,
    will bless the house of Aaron,

---

all praise to God. What is unusual is the absence of a reason for the people to have been praised in the first place. The second verse suggests an entirely different situation. The fact that other nations would ask, "Where is their God?" implies that the lot of the people was anything but praiseworthy or satisfying.

3-8 The worthlessness of foreign gods

A contrast is made between the sovereign majesty of Israel's God and the worthlessness of the gods of the other nations. On the one hand, the God of Israel is the only deity who rules from heaven and whose will is accomplished. On the other hand, the gods of the nations are merely ineffective idols. They may have been made of precious materials, but they are the products of human industry; they have no power in themselves. Furthermore, those people who worship these idols and who expect that they will act mightily, will be as powerless as are these human artifacts.

9-11 Trust in the Lord

A kind of antiphonal litany in which three classes of Israelites are said to trust in the Lord: the house of Israel, the house of Aaron, and those who fear the Lord. (The verb forms are really present imperative rather than past, as many contemporary versions translate them.) The house of Israel probably includes the entire nation; the house of Aaron is the priests. Since fear of the Lord is the fundamental religious disposition of awe and reverence before God, those who possess this disposition would be the genuinely religious ones among the people. In each case, the Lord is their help and their source of safety.

¹³Will bless those who fear the
	LORD,
		small and great alike.
¹⁴May the LORD increase your
	number,
		yours and your descendants.
¹⁵May you be blessed by the LORD,
	maker of heaven and earth.
¹⁶The heavens belong to the LORD,
	but he has given the earth to the
		children of Adam.
¹⁷The dead do not praise the LORD,
	not all those go down into
		silence.
¹⁸It is we who bless the LORD,
	both now and forever.
Hallelujah!

Thanksgiving to God Who Saves from Death

116

I

¹I love the LORD, who listened
	to my voice in supplication,
²Who turned an ear to me
	on the day I called.
³I was caught by the cords of death;
	the snares of Sheol had seized
		me;
	I felt agony and dread.
⁴Then I called on the name of the
	LORD,
	"O LORD, save my life!"

12-15 Blessings from God

The psalmist declares that God will be mindful of the same categories of people and will bless them. It is significant that both small and great are mentioned; there is no class preference here. The psalmist next prays for blessings on the people, specifically in terms of increase in population. This blessing extends across generations, from descendants to descendants. This invocation is made to the mighty God who is the creator of heaven and earth.

16-18 The living bless the Lord

The psalmist acknowledges that earth is the stage on which human beings enact the drama of life. Though they believed that God rules over both the heavens and the earth, they did not have a clear idea of God's control over the realm of the dead, and so they could not envision the dead praising God. Therefore, praise would come from the heavens and from the earth. It is the latter praise that was the responsibility of human beings. The psalm ends with just such praise: "Hallelujah!"

Psalm 116 (prayer of thanksgiving of an individual)

1-4 God heard my cry

The psalmist responds with love to God who has heard the psalmist's cries for help. The ancient Israelites considered any form of serious distress as some dimension of destruction or death. Therefore, to say that one was seized by death or by Sheol meant that one was afflicted with some form of grievous suffering, one that might eventually result in death, though not

<table>
<tr><td>II</td><td>III</td></tr>
</table>

II	III
[5]Gracious is the LORD and righteous; yes, our God is merciful. [6]The LORD protects the simple; I was helpless, but he saved me. [7]Return, my soul, to your rest; the LORD has been very good to you. [8]For my soul has been freed from death, my eyes from tears, my feet from stumbling. [9]I shall walk before the LORD in the land of the living.	[10]I kept faith, even when I said, "I am greatly afflicted!" [11]I said in my alarm, "All men are liars!" [12]How can I repay the LORD for all the great good done for me? [13]I will raise the cup of salvation and call on the name of the LORD. [14]I will pay my vows to the LORD in the presence of all his people. [15]Dear in the eyes of the LORD is the death of his devoted.

necessarily. It was from such a desperate predicament that the psalmist cried to God for help and was ultimately saved by God.

5-9 The graciousness of God

The graciousness and compassion of God's covenant commitment are coupled with fundamental divine justice. These dispositions have been turned toward those who are needy. The declaration itself is not impartial; the psalmist speaks from personal experience, having been the beneficiary of God's gracious care. There is no word in Hebrew for "soul." The word used might be better rendered "life force," a concept that is less abstract and thus makes this mysterious force more accessible to human under-standing. It is the psalmist's entire vital being that has been freed and is now called to turn to God in thanksgiving.

10-11 Suffering alone

The psalmist claims to have been faithful to and trusting of God, even during past times of great distress. At such times, no one but God offered help; no one but God served as refuge. Now, having been rescued from harm, the psalmist promises to continue to live a life of faithfulness.

12-19 A life of fidelity

Out of gratitude for having been saved from distress, the psalmist chooses a life of total commitment to the Lord. This promise will be partially accomplished through public acts of worship. It was a common devotional practice to promise some kind of offering if prayers were heard. The psalm-ist's public thanksgiving sacrifice would be the fulfillment of such a vow. The cup of salvation is probably part of a thanksgiving offering (cf. Num 28:7). God had saved the life of the psalmist, and now, in the midst of other

16LORD, I am your servant,
   your servant, the child of your
      maidservant;
   you have loosed my bonds.
17I will offer a sacrifice of praise
   and call on the name of the
      LORD.
18I will pay my vows to the LORD
   in the presence of all his people,
19In the courts of the house of the
      LORD,
   in your midst, O Jerusalem.
Hallelujah!

The Nations Called To Praise

117 1Praise the LORD, all you na-
      tions!
   Extol him, all you peoples!
2His mercy for us is strong;
   the faithfulness of the LORD is
      forever.
Hallelujah!

Hymn of Thanksgiving

118

I

1Give thanks to the LORD, for he is
      good,
   his mercy endures forever.
2Let Israel say:
   his mercy endures forever.
3Let the house of Aaron say,
   his mercy endures forever.
4Let those who fear the LORD say,
   his mercy endures forever.

II

5In danger I called on the LORD;
   the LORD answered me and set
      me free.
6The LORD is with me; I am not
      afraid;
   what can mortals do against
      me?

---

worshipers, the psalmist acknowledges God's graciousness. The psalm
ends on a note of praise: Praise (*hallel*) the Lord (*jah*)!

Psalm 117 (hymn)

1-2 Praise of God's love

This is the shortest psalm in the entire Psalter. Despite this brevity, it
contains the basic structure of a hymn, opening with a call to praise God.
This is a universal call, issued not only to Israel but to all nations, all peoples.
True to the hymnic structure, the reason for praise is given. God has acted
out of covenant love and faithfulness. Finally, the psalm ends as it began:
Praise (*hallel*) the Lord (*jah*)!

Psalm 118 (prayer of thanksgiving of an individual)

1-4 Give thanks

This summons to give thanks to God is in the form of antiphonal prayer
("his mercy endures forever"). The same categories of people are called on
as are found in Psalm 115. The house of Israel represents the entire nation;
the house of Aaron includes the priests; those who fear the Lord are the

⁷The LORD is with me as my helper;
    I shall look in triumph on my
        foes.
⁸Better to take refuge in the LORD
    than to put one's trust in mortals.
⁹Better to take refuge in the LORD
    than to put one's trust in
        princes.

they burned up like fire among
    thorns;
in the LORD's name I cut them
    off.
¹³I was hard pressed and falling,
    but the LORD came to my help.
¹⁴The LORD, my strength and might,
    has become my savior.

III

¹⁰All the nations surrounded me;
    in the LORD's name I cut them
        off.
¹¹They surrounded me on every
    side;
    in the LORD's name I cut them
        off.
¹²They surrounded me like bees;

IV

¹⁵The joyful shout of deliverance
    is heard in the tents of the
        righteous:
"The LORD's right hand works
    valiantly;
¹⁶the LORD's right hand is raised;
    the LORD's right hand works
        valiantly."

---

most devout. All of these people have acknowledged and responded to God's covenant love, a love that is unfailing and will last forever. They are now called on to demonstrate their gratitude for God's goodness.

5-9 The psalmist's testimony

The psalmist recalls past troublesome times when God was the only sure source of refuge. God's deliverance enabled the psalmist to realize that no human being could be trusted, not even the royalty whose responsibility it was to safeguard the populace. Only God was dependable; only God was a firm defense against threatening enemies; only God could be trusted.

10-18 Victory over enemies

Once again the psalmist employs an antiphonal prayer ("in the LORD's name I cut them off"). Though the psalmist fought the enemies, it was the power of God working through the psalmist that triumphed. The victory is really God's. The enemies are compared to a swarm of bees, surrounding and attacking the poor victim from every side. But the Lord delivered the psalmist from the sting of their fire. Besides describing God as a strong and mighty savior, the psalmist uses powerful military images to characterize God's defense. The tents are probably the military encampment; God's raised right hand is the hand that wields the weapon with which God will

¹⁷I shall not die but live
and declare the deeds of the
Lord.
¹⁸The Lord chastised me harshly,
but did not hand me over to
death.

V

¹⁹Open the gates of righteousness;
I will enter and thank the Lord.
²⁰This is the Lord's own gate,
through it the righteous enter.
²¹I thank you for you answered me;
you have been my savior.
²²The stone the builders rejected
has become the cornerstone.
²³By the Lord has this been done;
it is wonderful in our eyes.
²⁴This is the day the Lord has
made;
let us rejoice in it and be glad.

²⁵Lord, grant salvation!
Lord, grant good fortune!

VI

²⁶Blessed is he
who comes in the name of the
Lord.
We bless you from the house of the
Lord.
²⁷The Lord is God and has
enlightened us.
Join in procession with leafy
branches
up to the horns of the altar.

VII

²⁸You are my God, I give you thanks;
my God, I offer you praise.
²⁹Give thanks to the Lord, for he is
good,
his mercy endures forever.

---

frighten or even slay the psalmist's enemies. Without divine assistance the psalmist would have succumbed to the enemies' advances. God intervened, however, and for this the psalmist is grateful.

19-29 Thanksgiving liturgy

What follows is the description of a liturgical celebration of thanksgiving. The liturgy begins at the gates of the sanctuary, where thanks for deliverance is given. The psalmist acknowledges having been rejected by enemies, but saved by God and raised up in importance. This day of celebration is a day of divine victory, which gives it its significance. Though the celebration is for the rescue of the psalmist, all people are invited to rejoice in the salvation wrought by God. Throughout this liturgy, communal petitions for deliverance and blessing are directed to God. What follows is a form of liturgical dialogue. The one who comes in the name of the Lord is probably the priest who gives the blessing (v. 26). The people respond with a shout of praise and an invitation to proceed to the altar. The psalm concludes with the psalmist's words of thanksgiving and the repetition of the summons to give thanks that was issued at the beginning of the psalm.

A Prayer to God, the Lawgiver

119

Aleph

¹Blessed those whose way is
  blameless,
  who walk by the law of the
  LORD.
²Blessed those who keep his
  testimonies,
  who seek him with all their
  heart.
³They do no wrong;
  they walk in his ways.
⁴You have given them the command
  to observe your precepts with
  care.
⁵May my ways be firm
  in the observance of your
  statutes!

⁶Then I will not be ashamed
  to ponder all your
  commandments.
⁷I will praise you with sincere heart
  as I study your righteous
  judgments.
⁸I will observe your statutes;
  do not leave me all alone.

Beth

⁹How can the young keep his way
  without fault?
  Only by observing your words.
¹⁰With all my heart I seek you;
  do not let me stray from your
  commandments.
¹¹In my heart I treasure your
  promise,
  that I may not sin against you.
¹²Blessed are you, O LORD;
  teach me your statutes.

Psalm 119 (wisdom psalm)

This psalm is extraordinary not merely because of its length but also for its elaborate structure and the singular focus of its content. Like other acrostic psalms, it follows the alphabet sequence. However, where other such poems consist of twenty-two lines or verses, each beginning with a successive letter of the alphabet, this psalm is made up of sections of eight lines, each of which begins with the same letter. The psalm itself has one basic theme, the celebration of the law. There is no mistaking this praise, for each of the one hundred seventy-six verses acclaims the law and contains either the word *torah* (law) itself or a synonym of it. This group of synonyms includes words such as: way, teaching, decree, command, precepts, edict, word. Exaltation of the law is not an example of legalism. Actually, the word *torah* might be better translated "instruction." This rendering helps us to understand better the law as the fundamental teaching about life. It helps us to set our sights in the direction that will lead to success and happiness. Such an approach is certainly not legalistic.

Each section of the psalm contains basically the same focus. In order to avoid excessive repetition this reflection will address the salient theological themes found throughout the verses as well as some of its important literary characteristics. It will not present a section-by-section commentary.

¹³With my lips I recite
    all the judgments you have
      spoken.
¹⁴I find joy in the way of your
    testimonies
    more than in all riches.
¹⁵I will ponder your precepts
    and consider your paths.
¹⁶In your statutes I take delight;
    I will never forget your word.

Gimel
¹⁷Be kind to your servant that I may
    live,
    that I may keep your word.
¹⁸Open my eyes to see clearly
    the wonders of your law.
¹⁹I am a sojourner in the land;
    do not hide your command-
      ments from me.

²⁰At all times my soul is stirred
    with longing for your judgments.
²¹With a curse you rebuke the
    proud
    who stray from your command-
      ments.
²²Free me from disgrace and con-
    tempt,
    for I keep your testimonies.
²³Though princes meet and talk
    against me,
    your servant meditates on your
      statutes.
²⁴Your testimonies are my delight;
    they are my counselors.

Daleth
²⁵My soul clings to the dust;
    give me life in accord with your
      word.

Wisdom psalms are usually instruction rather than prayer. Still, this wisdom psalm contains elements of other genres as well. There are prayers of petition through the entire psalm (vv. 5, 66), as well as rhetorical questions used as a pedagogical device (v. 9), words of praise (v. 120), and cries of lament (v. 28, 84).

The acrostic structure is a familiar characteristic of the wisdom poetry. It is a mnemonic device, providing a recognizable pattern for data retention. Since it consists of the entire alphabet, the structure itself suggests a universal sweep that encompasses the entire range of a particular issue, everything from *alef* to *taw*, or from A to Z. In other words, Psalm 119 tells us what we need to know about observing the law of the Lord.

The psalm opens with a double beatitude (vv. 1-2), which sets the tone of the entire poem. This introductory acclamation indicates that observance of the law of the Lord is not a heavy burden. Rather, it is the source of true happiness. As is the case with much of the wisdom teaching, this perspective is based on an understanding of a form of cause and effect or the theory of retribution: wise or righteous living will result in happiness or reward; unhappiness or punishment will follow a foolish or wicked way of life. Wisdom teaching generally, and this treatise on observance of the law of the Lord in particular, provides a way of living that is both pleasing to God and will lead to happiness and success.

²⁶I disclosed my ways and you
answered me;
teach me your statutes.
²⁷Make me understand the way of
your precepts;
I will ponder your wondrous
deeds.
²⁸My soul is depressed;
lift me up acccording to your
word.
²⁹Lead me from the way of deceit;
favor me with your law.
³⁰The way of loyalty I have chosen;
I have kept your judgments.
³¹I cling to your testimonies, LORD;
do not let me come to shame.
³²I will run the way of your
commandments,
for you will broaden my heart.

He
³³LORD, teach me the way of your
statutes;
I shall keep them with care.
³⁴Give me understanding to keep
your law,
to observe it with all my heart.
³⁵Lead me in the path of your
commandments,
for that is my delight.
³⁶Direct my heart toward your
testimonies
and away from gain.
³⁷Avert my eyes from what is
worthless;
by your way give me life.
³⁸For your servant, fulfill your
promise
made to those who fear you.
³⁹Turn away from me the taunts I
dread,

for your judgments are good.
⁴⁰See how I long for your precepts;
in your righteousness give me
life.

Waw
⁴¹Let your mercy come to me, LORD,
salvation in accord with your
promise.
⁴²Let me answer my taunters with a
word,
for I trust in your word.
⁴³Do not take the word of truth
from my mouth,
for in your judgments is my
hope.
⁴⁴I will keep your law always,
for all time and forever.
⁴⁵I will walk freely in an open space
because I cherish your precepts.
⁴⁶I will speak openly of your
testimonies
without fear even before kings.
⁴⁷I delight in your commandments,
which I dearly love.
⁴⁸I lift up my hands to your
commandments;
I study your statutes, which I
love.

Zayin
⁴⁹Remember your word to your
servant
by which you give me hope.
⁵⁰This is my comfort in affliction,
your promise that gives me life.
⁵¹Though the arrogant utterly scorn
me,
I do not turn from your law.
⁵²When I recite your judgments of
old

Emphasis on law should be placed within the context of covenant. The psalmist is consistently identified as the servant of God (vv. 17, 23, 38, 49, 65, 76, 84, 124, 125, 135, 140, 176). This servant prays for and is enriched by the covenant attributes: mercy ("steadfast love" or "kindness" in other

I am comforted, LORD.
⁵³Rage seizes me because of the
   wicked;
   they forsake your law.
⁵⁴Your statutes become my songs
   wherever I make my home.
⁵⁵Even at night I remember your
   name
   in observance of your law, LORD.
⁵⁶This is my good fortune,
   for I have kept your precepts.

Heth
⁵⁷My portion is the LORD;
   I promise to observe your
   words.
⁵⁸I entreat you with all my heart:
   have mercy on me in accord
   with your promise.
⁵⁹I have examined my ways
   and turned my steps to your
   testimonies.
⁶⁰I am prompt, I do not hesitate
   in observing your commandments.
⁶¹Though the snares of the wicked
   surround me,
   your law I do not forget.
⁶²At midnight I rise to praise you
   because of your righteous
   judgments.
⁶³I am the friend of all who fear
   you,
   of all who observe your precepts.
⁶⁴The earth, LORD, is filled with
   your mercy;
   teach me your statutes.

Teth
⁶⁵You have treated your servant
   well,

according to your word, O
   LORD.
⁶⁶Teach me wisdom and knowledge,
   for in your commandments I
   trust.
⁶⁷Before I was afflicted I went
   astray,
   but now I hold to your promise.
⁶⁸You are good and do what is
   good;
   teach me your statutes.
⁶⁹The arrogant smear me with lies,
   but I keep your precepts with all
   my heart.
⁷⁰Their hearts are gross and fat;
   as for me, your law is my
   delight.
⁷¹It was good for me to be afflicted,
   in order to learn your statutes.
⁷²The law of your mouth is more
   precious to me
   than heaps of silver and gold.

Yodh
⁷³Your hands made me and
   fashioned me;
   give me understanding to learn
   your commandments.
⁷⁴Those who fear you rejoice to see
   me,
   because I hope in your word.
⁷⁵I know, LORD, that your judgments
   are righteous;
   though you afflict me, you are
   faithful.
⁷⁶May your mercy comfort me
   in accord with your promise to
   your servant.
⁷⁷Show me compassion that I may
   live,
   for your law is my delight.

---

translations; vv. 41, 64, 76, 88, 124, 149), compassion (v. 77, 156), and truth (vv. 43, 142).

This wisdom psalm exhibits a definite attitude of docility, a desire to be taught and to be led along the way of fidelity. Though wisdom grows out

⁷⁸Shame the proud for leading me
    astray with falsehood,
  that I may study your
    testimonies.
⁷⁹Let those who fear you turn to me,
  those who acknowledge your
    testimonies.
⁸⁰May I be wholehearted toward
    your statutes,
  that I may not be put to shame.

Kaph
⁸¹My soul longs for your salvation;
  I put my hope in your word.
⁸²My eyes long to see your promise.
  When will you comfort me?
⁸³I am like a wineskin shriveled by
    smoke,
  but I have not forgotten your
    statutes.
⁸⁴How long can your servant
    survive?
  When will your judgment doom
    my foes?
⁸⁵The arrogant have dug pits for me;
  defying your law.
⁸⁶All your commandments are
    steadfast.
  Help me! I am pursued without
    cause.
⁸⁷They have almost put an end to
    me on earth,
  but I do not forsake your
    precepts.
⁸⁸In your mercy give me life,
  to observe the testimonies of
    your mouth.

Lamedh
⁸⁹Your word, Lord, stands forever;
  it is firm as the heavens.

⁹⁰Through all generations your
    truth endures;
  fixed to stand firm like the earth.
⁹¹By your judgments they stand
    firm to this day,
  for all things are your servants.
⁹²Had your law not been my
    delight,
  I would have perished in my
    affliction.
⁹³I will never forget your precepts;
  through them you give me life.
⁹⁴I am yours; save me,
  for I cherish your precepts.
⁹⁵The wicked hope to destroy me,
  but I seek to understand your
    testimonies.
⁹⁶I have seen the limits of all
    perfection,
  but your commandment is
    without bounds.

Mem
⁹⁷How I love your law, Lord!
  I study it all day long.
⁹⁸Your commandment makes me
    wiser than my foes,
  as it is forever with me.
⁹⁹I have more insight than all my
    teachers,
  because I ponder your
    testimonies.
¹⁰⁰I have more understanding than
    my elders,
  because I keep your precepts.
¹⁰¹I keep my steps from every evil
    path,
  that I may observe your word.
¹⁰²From your judgments I do not
    turn,
  for you have instructed me.

---

of reflection on life experience, this psalm clearly underscores the need to
be led by God (vv. 12, 29, 33, 66, 171). The law is not only a list of precepts
to be obeyed but, more important, it is a way of life to be studied (vv. 97-
100). The psalmist prays not only for obedience but also for insight (vv. 27,

¹⁰³How sweet to my tongue is your
    promise,
    sweeter than honey to my
        mouth!
¹⁰⁴Through your precepts I gain
    understanding;
    therefore I hate all false ways.

Nun

¹⁰⁵Your word is a lamp for my feet,
    a light for my path.
¹⁰⁶I make a solemn vow
    to observe your righteous
        judgments.
¹⁰⁷I am very much afflicted, LORD;
    give me life in accord with your
        word.
¹⁰⁸Accept my freely offered praise;
    LORD, teach me your judgments.
¹⁰⁹My life is always at risk,
    but I do not forget your law.
¹¹⁰The wicked have set snares for me,
    but from your precepts I do not
        stray.
¹¹¹Your testimonies are my heritage
    forever;
    they are the joy of my heart.
¹¹²My heart is set on fulfilling your
    statutes;
    they are my reward forever.

Samekh

¹¹³I hate every hypocrite;
    your law I love.
¹¹⁴You are my refuge and shield;
    in your word I hope.
¹¹⁵Depart from me, you wicked,
    that I may keep the command-
        ments of my God.

¹¹⁶Sustain me by your promise that I
    may live;
    do not disappoint me in my
        hope.
¹¹⁷Strengthen me that I may be safe,
    ever to contemplate your
        statutes.
¹¹⁸You reject all who stray from your
    statutes,
    for vain is their deceit.
¹¹⁹Like dross you regard all the
    wicked on earth;
    therefore I love your testimonies.
¹²⁰My flesh shudders with dread of
    you;
    I fear your judgments.

Ayin

¹²¹I have fulfilled your righteous
    judgment;
    do not abandon me to my
        oppressors.
¹²²Guarantee your servant's welfare;
    do not let the arrogant oppress
        me.
¹²³My eyes long to see your salvation
    and the promise of your
        righteousness.
¹²⁴Act with mercy toward your
    servant;
    teach me your statutes.
¹²⁵I am your servant; give me
    discernment
    that I may know your
        testimonies.
¹²⁶It is time for the LORD to act;
    they have disobeyed your law.
¹²⁷Truly I love your commandments
    more than gold, more than the
        finest gold.

34, 104) and direction (vv. 18, 35). Furthermore, a life lived in accordance
with the law is often ridiculed by others (vv. 39, 51, 141). In the eyes of the
psalmist, these others would be considered foolish. Nonetheless, their derision is difficult to endure, so the psalmist also prays for the fortitude needed

128Thus, I follow all your precepts;
    every wrong way I hate.

Pe

129Wonderful are your testimonies;
    therefore I keep them.
130The revelation of your words
        sheds light,
    gives understanding to the
        simple.
131I sigh with open mouth,
    yearning for your command-
        ments.
132Turn to me and be gracious,
    according to your judgment for
        those who love your
        name.
133Steady my feet in accord with
        your promise;
    do not let iniquity lead me.
134Free me from human oppression,
    that I may observe your precepts.
135Let your face shine upon your
        servant;
    teach me your statutes.
136My eyes shed streams of tears
    because your law is not observed.

Sadhe

137You are righteous, LORD,
    and just are your judgments.
138You have given your testimonies
        in righteousness
    and in surpassing faithfulness.
139I am consumed with rage,
    because my foes forget your
        words.
140Your servant loves your promise;
    it has been proved by fire.
141Though belittled and despised,

I do not forget your precepts.
142Your justice is forever right,
    your law true.
143Though distress and anguish
        come upon me,
    your commandments are my
        delight.
144Your testimonies are forever
        righteous;
    give me understanding that I
        may live.
145I call with all my heart, O LORD;
    answer me that I may keep your
        statutes.
146I call to you to save me
    that I may observe your
        testimonies.
147I rise before dawn and cry out;
    I put my hope in your words.
148My eyes greet the night watches
    as I meditate on your promise.
149Hear my voice in your mercy, O
        LORD;
    by your judgment give me life.
150Malicious persecutors draw near
        me;
    they are far from your law.
151You are near, O LORD;
    reliable are all your command-
        ments.
152Long have I known from your
        testimonies
    that you have established them
        forever.

Resh

153Look at my affliction and rescue
        me,
    for I have not forgotten your
        law.

to remain faithful in the face of such a trial. The psalmist is dependent on God for deliverance from hardship as well as direction for living. Enemies had oppressed the psalmist who had nowhere to turn but to the Lord (vv. 81-88, 121, 153-155, 161).

"Your word is a lamp for my feet, a light for my path" (Ps 119:105).

¹⁵⁴Take up my cause and redeem
  me;
    for the sake of your promise
    give me life.
¹⁵⁵Salvation is far from sinners
    because they do not cherish
    your statutes.
¹⁵⁶Your compassion is great, O
  LORD;
    in accord with your judgments,
    give me life.
¹⁵⁷Though my persecutors and foes
  are many,
    I do not turn from your
    testimonies.
¹⁵⁸I view the faithless with loathing
    because they do not heed your
    promise.
¹⁵⁹See how I love your precepts,
  LORD;
    in your mercy give me life.
¹⁶⁰Your every word is enduring;
    all your righteous judgments are
    forever.

Shin
¹⁶¹Princes persecute me without
  reason,
    but my heart reveres only your
    word.
¹⁶²I rejoice at your promise,
    as one who has found rich spoil.
¹⁶³Falsehood I hate and abhor;
    your law I love.
¹⁶⁴Seven times a day I praise you
    because your judgments are
    righteous.
¹⁶⁵Lovers of your law have much
  peace;

for them there is no stumbling
  block.
¹⁶⁶I look for your salvation, LORD,
    and I fulfill your command-
    ments.
¹⁶⁷I observe your testimonies;
    I love them very much.
¹⁶⁸I observe your precepts and
    testimonies;
    all my ways are before you.

Taw
¹⁶⁹Let my cry come before you,
  LORD;
    in keeping with your word, give
    me understanding.
¹⁷⁰Let my prayer come before you;
    rescue me according to your
    promise.
¹⁷¹May my lips pour forth your
  praise,
    because you teach me your
    statutes.
¹⁷²May my tongue sing of your
  promise,
    for all your commandments are
    righteous.
¹⁷³Keep your hand ready to help
  me,
    for I have chosen your precepts.
¹⁷⁴I long for your salvation, LORD;
    your law is my delight.
¹⁷⁵Let my soul live to praise you;
    may your judgments give me
    help.
¹⁷⁶I have wandered like a lost sheep;
    seek out your servant,
    for I do not forget your
    commandments.

Although the psalm opens with a clearly defined poetic device (beatitude), it closes rather abruptly. The acrostic pattern has been faithfully
followed and so there is nothing left to say.

Prayer of a Returned Exile

120 ¹A song of ascents.

The LORD answered me
  when I called in my distress:
²LORD, deliver my soul from lying
  lips,
    from a treacherous tongue.

³What will he inflict on you,
  O treacherous tongue,
    and what more besides?
⁴A warrior's arrows
  sharpened with coals of brush
    wood!
⁵Alas, I am a foreigner in Meshech,
  I live among the tents of Kedar!

SONGS OF ASCENT (120–34)

Although the next fifteen psalms are classified according to various standard genres, they comprise a discrete collection known as the Songs of Ascent. Most likely they were used during the pilgrimage to Jerusalem on the occasion of the major festivals. Some commentators suggest when and how these psalms might have been part of religious pilgrimages to the holy city. However, many of the psalms lack explicit references to such processions. In this commentary, whatever connections there might be to historical events will be made only when features within the psalm itself warrant them.

Psalm 120 (composite psalm)

1-2 Deliverance from enemies

Commentators debate the relationship between these two verses. Some say that the second verse is dependent on the first—that it is the prayer that was offered by the psalmist and heard by God. This would mean that the psalmist has been delivered and endures as a freed person. Others maintain that the verses are independent of each other. This reading would imply that the psalmist was delivered in the past, but that this prayer springs from yet another situation of distress. Whichever version is the case, the fundamental meaning is the same: The psalmist was besieged by liars and God stepped in as deliverer.

3-4 The fate of the liars

The psalmist turns to the liars themselves and challenges them. What have they gained from their deceit? In punishment for their sins, they will become the victims of the sharp weapons of their own enemies.

5-7 A lament

The psalm ends with a lament. The psalmist cries out in the traditional form of woe: "Alas!" The psalmist, who cherishes peace, is forced to live

⁶Too long do I live
  among those who hate peace.
⁷When I speak of peace,
  they are for war.

The Lord My Guardian

121 ¹A song of ascents.

I raise my eyes toward the
  mountains.
  From whence shall come my
    help?
²My help comes from the LORD,
  the maker of heaven and earth.

³He will not allow your foot to slip;
  or your guardian to sleep.
⁴Behold, the guardian of Israel
  never slumbers nor sleeps.
⁵The LORD is your guardian;
  the LORD is your shade
  at your right hand.
⁶By day the sun will not strike you,
  nor the moon by night.
⁷The LORD will guard you from all
  evil;
  he will guard your soul.
⁸The LORD will guard your coming
  and going
  both now and forever.

---

as an alien among people committed to war. Meshech was land in the distant northeast, between the Black and the Caspian Seas; Kedar was an Arabian tribe that lived in tents in the southeast.

Psalm 121 (prayer of confidence of an individual)

1-2 God is a sure refuge

The initial scene envisioned is that of the psalmist either on flat land or in a valley, somewhat defenseless, looking toward the mountains for help. The identification of God as the maker of heaven and earth suggests that these are cosmic mountains on which God dwells and from which God comes to save.

3-8 The divine guardian

An unknown voice addresses the psalmist, designating God as a watchful and constant guardian. To underscore this characterization of God, the author uses some form of the word "guard" no less than six times in this short psalm (vv. 3, 4, 5, 7 [2x], 8). There are dangers in the psalmist's "coming and going." With God as guardian, however, the psalmist is guaranteed sure footing. Besides being a dependable guardian, God is described as ever-watchful, protective in the face of heat, and a source of strength ("right hand"). Reference to the sun and moon, revered by ancient Near Eastern people as celestial deities, could have cosmic significance. However, this may also be a poetic way of claiming that neither dangers of the day nor those of the night will have any power over the one who is guarded by God.

A Pilgrim's Prayer for Jerusalem

122 ¹A song of ascents. Of David.

I

I rejoiced when they said to me,
    "Let us go to the house of the
        LORD."
²And now our feet are standing
    within your gates, Jerusalem.
³Jerusalem, built as a city,
    walled round about.
⁴There the tribes go up,
    the tribes of the LORD,
As it was decreed for Israel,
    to give thanks to the name of the
        LORD.

⁵There are the thrones of justice,
    the thrones of the house of
        David.

II

⁶For the peace of Jerusalem pray:
    "May those who love you
        prosper!
⁷May peace be within your ramparts,
    prosperity within your towers."
⁸For the sake of my brothers and
        friends I say,
    "Peace be with you."
⁹For the sake of the house of the
        LORD, our God,
I pray for your good.

Psalm 122 (song of Zion)

1-5 Pilgrimage to the temple

The theme of pilgrimage is explicit in this psalm. Having been invited to join a procession to the temple in Jerusalem, the psalmist stands within that city, overwhelmed by his good fortune to have come to this place of both religious and political significance, and by the glory of the city itself. Like most important ancient settlements, Jerusalem was a walled city with carefully protected gates. It was the renowned seat of Davidic rule, the place where justice was meted out to all. The political grandeur of this city notwithstanding, the psalmist's visit was religiously motivated. All Israelites were required to make religious pilgrimage to Jerusalem to offer thanks to God there. It was for this reason that the psalmist made the journey.

6-9 A prayer for peace

There are three distinct prayers for the peace of Jerusalem, the city whose very name in Hebrew contains the root letters for the word "peace" (*shalom*). The first prayer is for peace for those who are favorably disposed toward the city. The second is that peace might reign within the city itself. The third prayer for peace is for family and friends. This may refer to those unable to make the pilgrimage. These prayers are for peace in the broadest sense, not merely for the absence of conflict. Such peace is really a state of wholeness and contentment, of fulfillment and prosperity. Jerusalem, chosen and blessed by God, was a symbol of this all-encompassing peace and a sign of promise for all those who traveled to it on religious pilgrimage.

Reliance on the Lord

123 ¹A song of ascents.

To you I raise my eyes,
    to you enthroned in heaven.
²Yes, like the eyes of servants
    on the hand of their masters,
Like the eyes of a maid
    on the hand of her mistress,
So our eyes are on the LORD our
    God,
    till we are shown favor.
³Show us favor, LORD, show us
    favor,
    for we have our fill of contempt.
⁴Our souls are more than sated
    with mockery from the insolent,
with contempt from the
    arrogant.

God, the Rescuer of the People

124 ¹A song of ascents. Of David.

Had not the LORD been with us,
    let Israel say,
²Had not the LORD been with us,
    when people rose against us,
³Then they would have swallowed
    us alive,
    for their fury blazed against us.
⁴Then the waters would have
    engulfed us,
    the torrent overwhelmed us;
⁵then seething water would
    have drowned us.

Psalm 123 (communal lament)

1 Individual cry

The psalmist speaks in the singular. To raise one's eyes is to look for help. The psalmist looks for help from God who reigns as sovereign from heaven.

2-4 Communal cry

The psalmist develops further the theme of eyes, now speaking for the entire community. The comparisons employed are drawn from the social practice of servitude. As male and female servants look for blessings from the hands of their master and mistress respectively, so the people look to God. The cry for blessing is repeated twice. One must wait until the end of the psalm to discover the reason why the people turn to God for help. They have been the victims of the contempt of others. Now they turn to God for release.

Psalm 124 (communal prayer of thanksgiving)

1-5 Rescued by God

The psalmist describes how the people were rescued by God from the assaults of others. The serious jeopardy in which they found themselves is captured in the metaphors used to describe the fate that would have been theirs had they been vanquished. They would have been swallowed alive,

115

"And now our feet are standing within your gates, Jerusalem. Jerusalem, built as a city, walled round about" (Ps 122:2-3).

⁶Blessed is the LORD, who did not
leave us
to be torn by their teeth.
⁷We escaped with our lives like a
bird
from the fowler's snare;
the snare was broken,
and we escaped.
⁸Our help is in the name of the
LORD,
the maker of heaven and earth.

Israel's Protector

125 ¹A song of ascents.

Those trusting in the LORD are like
Mount Zion,
unshakable, forever enduring.
²As mountains surround Jerusalem,
the LORD surrounds his people
both now and forever.
³The scepter of the wicked will not
prevail
in the land allotted to the just,

---

engulfed by waters, swept away, and finally drowned. The choice of water imagery is significant, for water was the symbol of primordial chaos. Used here, it emphasizes both the ferocity of the enemies' attack and the character of the marvelous victory wrought by God.

6-8 Praise of God

The psalmist praises God for having rescued the people from their enemies. The imagery employed to describe this rescue has been borrowed from hunting practices. No longer are the people threatened by water. Here they face the possibility of being the prey of fierce animals or human hunters; however, God, who is the maker of heaven and earth, saved them from being ripped apart. God broke the snare that had entangled them and set them free.

Psalm 125 (communal prayer of confidence)

1-2 Trust in God

According to this psalm, those who trust God are guaranteed a security that is as grounded as the mountains. Israel claimed that Mount Zion, the very hill on which Jerusalem was built, was firmly established by God from the very beginning. By means of a different but related image of mountains, the psalmist then compares God's encircling protection to the mountains that surround Mount Zion and Jerusalem. Twice the psalmist states that such divine security will last forever.

3 Secure from the wicked

Security in the land, free from the rule of the wicked, is granted the just in order that they not fall under the influence of the wicked and turn to wickedness themselves.

Lest the just themselves
    turn their hands to evil.
4Do good, Lord, to the good,
    to those who are upright of
      heart.
5But those who turn aside to
    crooked ways
    may the Lord send down with
      the evildoers.
Peace upon Israel!

The Reversal of Zion's Fortunes

126 1A song of ascents.

I

When the Lord restored the
    captives of Zion,
    we thought we were dreaming.
2Then our mouths were filled with
    laughter;
    our tongues sang for joy.
Then it was said among the nations,
    "The Lord had done great
      things for them."
3The Lord has done great things for
    us;
    Oh, how happy we were!
4Restore our captives, Lord,
    like the dry stream beds of the
      Negeb.

4-5 Divine retribution

The psalmist prays for divine retribution, that the righteous be blessed by God and those who choose wickedness be made to endure the punishment meant for the wicked. The psalm closes with a wish that does not really flow from the sentiments expressed in earlier verses, but that is always relevant: Peace upon Israel!

Psalm 126 (communal lament)

1-3 Past deliverance

The people recall how, in the past, God restored the city that had been devastated. If this is a reference to the return to Jerusalem from Babylonian exile, the psalm might be dated in the postexilic period. This restoration was astounding. It amazed the delivered people themselves, and it became known throughout the world. Other nations marveled at the wonders God had worked for this people.

4-6 Present need

Relying on those past favors granted by God, the people pray again for the reversal of fortune. Some commentators maintain that the reference is to the same favor as mentioned above. However, here the people are not asking for deliverance, but for restoration in their homeland. The nature imagery is striking. The Negeb Desert is known for the sudden flooding of its riverbeds during the winter rains. It is for such remarkable reversals that the people pray. The agricultural image is not as easy to understand. It may have originated in the earlier Canaanite fertility cult. During that

II

5Those who sow in tears
    will reap with cries of joy.
6Those who go forth weeping,
    carrying sacks of seed,
Will return with cries of joy,
    carrying their bundled sheaves.

The Need of God's Blessing

127 1A song of ascents. Of Solomon.

I

Unless the LORD build the house,
    they labor in vain who build.
Unless the LORD guard the city,
    in vain does the guard keep
      watch.

2It is vain for you to rise early
    and put off your rest at night,
To eat bread earned by hard toil—
    all this God gives to his beloved
      in sleep.

II

3Certainly sons are a gift from the
    LORD,
    the fruit of the womb, a reward.
4Like arrows in the hand of a warrior
    are the sons born in one's youth.
5Blessed is the man who has filled
    his quiver with them.
He will never be shamed
    for he will destroy his foes at the
      gate.

---

ritual, the people weep at the time of sowing when the land appears to be lifeless, but rejoice at harvest when clearly that life has returned. Here this ancient rite suggests the death that the exile represented and the new life experienced at the people's return. The psalm seems to end abruptly.

Psalm 127 (wisdom psalm)

1-2 Limitations of human endeavor

The basis of wisdom is the insight into life that one gains through studious reflection on experience. Here the psalmist insists that the most important lesson that one could learn is the futility of every human endeavor pursued without direction from or the assistance of God. Building houses and guarding cities are simply representative of fundamental and necessary human ventures. Even the most basic activity of rising early to cultivate the land for food is considered useless, for it is really God who provides.

3-5 Children as a blessing

This society cherished its children, not simply out of emotional sentiment, but because they realized that children are the future of the nation. As with all other realities, they saw children as gifts from God. Children are also the defense (arrows) against whatever may be threatening. This could range from actual enemies to the diminishment that comes with aging. The psalm closes with a beatitude. It states that the one who has many children, who can ensure a prosperous future and care in old age, will be truly blessed.

The Blessed Home of the Just

128 ¹A song of ascents.

I

Blessed are all who fear the LORD,
and who walk in his ways.
²What your hands provide you will
enjoy;
you will be blessed and prosper:
³Your wife will be like a fruitful
vine
within your home,
Your children like young olive
plants
around your table.
⁴Just so will the man be blessed
who fears the LORD.

II

⁵May the LORD bless you from
Zion;
may you see Jerusalem's
prosperity
all the days of your life,
⁶and live to see your children's
children.
Peace upon Israel!

Against Israel's Enemies

129 ¹A song of ascents.

I

Viciously have they attacked me
from my youth,
let Israel say now.

Psalm 128 (wisdom psalm)

1-4 Fear of the Lord

This psalm opens with *the* beatitude: "Happy are all who fear the LORD." According to the wisdom tradition, this fear or awe before God is the fundamental religious attitude. Those who possess it follow the path set out for them by God. As a consequence, they will enjoy the rewards that come from such fidelity. While peace and prosperity are treasured blessings, the most meaningful blessing is children.

5-6 Words of blessing

The psalm ends with words of blessing. Zion or Jerusalem was the dwelling place of God on earth. It was from this hallowed place that God's blessings flowed. This final prayer consists of three petitions: that blessings will be granted throughout life; that those for whom the prayer is offered will share in the peace of Jerusalem; that they will enjoy a long life and see generations of descendants. The psalm ends with a prayer for peace for Jerusalem.

Psalm 129 (communal prayer of confidence)

1-4 Past deliverance

Although the psalmist speaks in the first person, the focus here is the deliverance experienced by the entire people. This is a nation that has been on the offensive from the very first days of its existence. Though assaulted,

119

²Viciously have they attacked me
from my youth,
yet they have not prevailed
against me.
³Upon my back the plowers
plowed,
as they traced their long furrows.
⁴But the just LORD cut me free
from the ropes of the wicked.

II

⁵May they recoil in disgrace,
all who hate Zion.
⁶May they be like grass on the roof-
tops
withered in early growth,
⁷Never to fill the reaper's hands,

nor the arms of the binders of
sheaves,
⁸And with none passing by to call
out:
"The blessing of the LORD be
upon you!
We bless you in the name of the
LORD!"

Prayer for Pardon and Mercy

130 ¹A song of ascents.

I

Out of the depths I call to you,
LORD;
²Lord, hear my cry!

however, it has not been vanquished. With a vivid agricultural image, the psalmist depicts its former servile condition and the pain that it endured because of it. However, God intervened on the nation's behalf and released it from its bondage.

5-8 Fate of the wicked

In the manner of a curse, the psalmist wishes ill fortune on those who hate God's holy city. The first misfortune that the psalmist would have fall on them is the burden of shame. In many societies, even today, shame is sometimes considered a suffering worse than death. In addition to this adversity, the psalmist would have these people dry up and shrivel like the grass in thatched roofs. When the dry and scorching winds sweep over the houses, the burned grass is made worthless. The psalmist would have this happen to the enemies. Finally, may they never hear words of blessing addressed to them. Those who have scorned what God loves do not deserve God's blessing. The psalm ends on this note of imprecation.

Psalm 130 (lament of an individual; penitential)

1-2 The lament

In this penitential psalm (cf. Pss 6, 32, 38, 51, 102, 143), the situation of the psalmist appears to be dire; "depths" refers to deepest suffering. It is from there that the psalmist cries out to God for mercy. This is not the mercy associated with the covenant. It is the kind of pity that one shows toward another who is in great distress. The psalmist begs that God will hear the cry and will respond with some kind of relief.

May your ears be attentive
    to my cry for mercy.
[3]If you, Lord, keep account of sins,
    Lord, who can stand?
[4]But with you is forgiveness
    and so you are revered.

II

[5]I wait for the Lord,
    my soul waits
    and I hope for his word.
[6]My soul looks for the Lord
    more than sentinels for daybreak.

More than sentinels for daybreak,
    [7]let Israel hope in the Lord,
For with the Lord is mercy,
    with him is plenteous
        redemption,
[8]And he will redeem Israel
    from all its sins.

Humble Trust in God

131 [1]A song of ascents. Of David.

Lord, my heart is not proud;
    nor are my eyes haughty.

3-4 A prayer for forgiveness

The psalmist does not ask for justice, but for forgiveness. Such a prayer suggests that this is not an innocent sufferer, but one who is guilty of some offense. In this prayer it is the mercy of God that is extolled, not divine justice.

5-6 A prayer of confidence

As is the case with so many psalms of lament, this prayer ends on a note of confidence. The psalmist has already acknowledged some degree of guilt and has appealed to God's mercy. There is nothing more to do but wait patiently and hopefully for God to respond. The vital life force waits for the Lord. The reference to dawn suggests that the long nightwatch is over. It also assures the sentinel that the terrors that fill the night will have no power in the light of day. The psalmist waits for God's mercy with the same degree of expectation.

7-8 Prayer for the community

The individual character of the psalm changes to one that is communal. Now it is the entire people who are urged to wait longingly for the Lord. The concept of covenant love is introduced, as is the notion of paying a ransom for another. It is God who will pay this ransom on Israel's behalf.

Psalm 131 (prayer of confidence of an individual)

1-3 Resting in the Lord

There is deep serenity in the words of the psalmist. A proud heart and haughty eyes are signs of great ambition, a trait that is absent in this humble individual. A weaned child is one whose hunger has been satisfied and who now rests contently at its mother's breast. This passage contains not

I do not busy myself with great
matters,
  with things too sublime for me.
²Rather, I have stilled my soul,
Like a weaned child to its mother,
  weaned is my soul.
³Israel, hope in the LORD,
  now and forever.

The Covenant Between David and God

132 ¹A song of ascents.

I

Remember, O LORD, for David
  all his hardships;

²How he swore an oath to the LORD,
  vowed to the Mighty One of
    Jacob:
³"I will not enter the house where I
  live,
  nor lie on the couch where I
    sleep;
⁴I will give my eyes no sleep,
  my eyelids no rest,
⁵Till I find a place for the LORD,
  a dwelling for the Mighty One
    of Jacob."
⁶"We have heard of it in Ephrathah;
  we have found it in the fields of
    Jaar.
⁷Let us enter his dwelling;
  let us worship at his footstool."

only a moving description of the psalmist but also a tender characterization of God—a mother who has given of her very self for the life of her child. Such an understanding of God surely generated trust in the hearts of the people. The psalm ends with a summons to such trust.

Psalm 132 (royal psalm)

1-5 David's oath

The first part of this psalm recalls David's plan to build a sanctuary for the Lord (cf. 2 Sam 7:1-2). Although the psalm suggests that this plan sprang from religious devotion, such a building project was expected of any successful ancient Near Eastern ruler. Therefore, political obligation was involved as well. The divine title "Mighty One of Jacob" is an ancient name for God. It is first found in the ancestral narrative (cf. Gen 49:24) and then, along with the designation "redeemer," in postexilic writings (cf. Isa 49:26; 60:16). Its inclusion in this psalm links the royal temple tradition with both the ancestral or tribal tradition and that of the postexilic prophet Deutero-Isaiah. This connection gives the temple tradition, which some within the community might have seen as a Canaanite innovation, both legitimation and continuity with more established religious traditions.

6-10 Liturgical procession

It is clear that temple worship has been established and the ark of the covenant, the religious symbol of God's presence in the midst of the people, has found a place within the sanctuary. The people are invited to join in

⁸"Arise, LORD, come to your resting place,
you and your mighty ark.
⁹Your priests will be clothed with justice;
your devout will shout for joy."
¹⁰For the sake of David your servant,
do not reject your anointed.

II

¹¹The LORD swore an oath to David in truth,
he will never turn back from it:
"Your own offspring I will set upon your throne.
¹²If your sons observe my covenant, and my decrees I shall teach them,
Their sons, in turn,
shall sit forever on your throne."
¹³Yes, the LORD has chosen Zion,
desired it for a dwelling:
¹⁴"This is my resting place forever; here I will dwell, for I desire it.
¹⁵I will bless Zion with provisions; its poor I will fill with bread.
¹⁶I will clothe its priests with salvation;
its devout shall shout for joy.
¹⁷There I will make a horn sprout for David;
I will set a lamp for my anointed.
¹⁸His foes I will clothe with shame, but on him his crown shall shine."

A Vision of a Blessed Community

133 ¹A song of ascents. Of David.

How good and how pleasant it is,
when brothers dwell together as one!

---

procession to the temple to celebrate either its dedication or the anniversary of that event. The psalmist calls on a well-established Davidic tradition and asks God to be mindful of the present king for the sake of the founder of the dynasty. The psalm includes other Davidic connections. Ephrathah is associated with Bethlehem, the city of David (cf. Mic 5:1). The fields of Jaar is a district west of Jerusalem near Bethlehem. It was there that the ark of the covenant was kept (cf. 1 Sam 7:1) before David brought it to Jerusalem (cf. 2 Sam 6:12).

11-18 The divine oath

The psalm recalls the oath that God made to David to establish the family of David as a royal dynasty (cf. 2 Sam 7:12-16). The covenant made at this time was considered eternal, from generation to generation. However, the reign of each individual ruler was dependent on his fidelity to the Mosaic law that bound every Israelite. Not only was the Davidic family specially chosen, but Jerusalem, the city of David, was also set apart as the place where God dwelt on earth. The oath contains a promise to grant the city choice blessings. The horn is a sign of the strength of the dynasty. The lamp may be a reference to the flask of oil that remained burning in the

²Like fine oil on the head,
    running down upon the beard,
Upon the beard of Aaron,
    upon the collar of his robe.
³Like dew of Hermon coming down
    upon the mountains of Zion.
There the LORD has decreed a
      blessing,
life for evermore!

**Exhortation to the Night Watch to
Bless God**

134 ¹A song of ascents.

O come, bless the LORD,
    all you servants of the LORD
You who stand in the house of the
    LORD
    throughout the nights.

---

temple. It is clear that the strength and endurance of the dynasty and the splendor of the temple are grounded in this promise of God.

Psalm 133 (wisdom psalm)

1-3 A harmonious community

The wisdom saying that comprises this psalm extols the blessings that accrue for a community that lives together in harmony. The saying includes two vivid images that describe this harmony, both of which rely on the belief that these blessings really come down to the people from God. The first image originates in the cultic ceremony of priestly anointing. The precious ointment that was poured over the head of the priest ran down his head and over his beard, its luxurious aroma filling the air. In like manner, the pleasurable scent of harmonious community living brings joy to all. The second image is drawn from Mount Hermon, which stands majestic in the northern part of Israel. The dew from its peaks flows down to the valleys below and there waters the land, making it fertile and productive. Similarly, harmonious community living is the source of many other blessings.

Psalm 134 (liturgical hymn)

1-3 A call to worship

The collection of songs of ascent (Pss 120–34) appropriately closes with a liturgical hymn. This prayer contains several ritual elements. It opens with a call to praise God. It takes place in the temple, after the long hours of a night vigil. Included is a directive to raise one's hands in prayer, a traditional stance of petition. It closes with a prayer for blessing from God, who is the creator of heaven and earth but who dwells in the temple in Jerusalem.

²Lift up your hands toward the
    sanctuary,
    and bless the LORD.
³May the LORD bless you from
    Zion,
    the Maker of heaven and earth.

Praise of God, the Ruler and Benefactor of Israel

135 ¹Hallelujah!

I

Praise the name of the LORD!
    Praise, you servants of the LORD,

²Who stand in the house of the
    LORD,
    in the courts of the house of our
    God!
³Praise the LORD, for the LORD is
    good!
    Sing to his name, for it brings
    joy!
⁴For the LORD has chosen Jacob for
    himself,
    Israel as his treasured possession.

II

⁵For I know that the LORD is great,
    that our Lord is greater than all
    gods.

Psalm 135 (hymn)

1-4 A summons to praise God

This hymn of praise opens with the traditional cry: "Hallelujah!" The call to praise either the Lord or the name of the Lord is repeated three times in this section. Many people believe that the name contains a dimension of the very essence of the person. Therefore, to praise God's name is to praise God. The house of the Lord is the sanctuary; the servants who stand in service in the sanctuary are probably the priests and Levites. They are called on to sing praise to God. Typical of the structure of the hymn, reason for praise is given: God has chosen Israel as a special people.

5-7 The superiority of the God of Israel

The psalmist continues to cite reasons for praising God. Israel's God is greater than all other gods, exercising dominion over the heavens and the earth alike. Seas and deeps are references to primordial chaotic waters. Many people of the ancient world believed that the great storm gods rode across the heavens in chariots of clouds, with bolts of lightning like arrows in their quivers. Here, such celestial phenomena are recognized as simple meteorological manifestations under God's supreme control.

8-14 God's salvific wonders

Israel's God is not only the creator but also a deliverer. A short account of God's salvific marvels is recited, beginning with a report of their deliverance from bondage in Egypt, the event that will forever mark Israel as God's chosen possession (cf. v. 4). This is followed by an allusion to the victories

◄

⁶Whatever the LORD desires
　　he does in heaven and on earth,
　　in the seas and all the depths.
⁷It is he who raises storm clouds
　　　from the end of the earth,
　　makes lightning for the rain,
　　and brings forth wind from his
　　　storehouse.

III

⁸He struck down Egypt's firstborn,
　　of human being and beast alike,
⁹And sent signs and wonders
　　against you, Egypt,
　　against Pharaoh and all his
　　　servants.
¹⁰It is he who struck down many
　　nations,
　　and slew mighty kings—
¹¹Sihon, king of the Amorites,
　　and Og, king of Bashan,
　　all the kings of Canaan—
¹²And made their land a heritage,
　　a heritage for Israel his people.

¹³O LORD, your name is forever,
　　your renown, from generation
　　　to generation!
¹⁴For the LORD defends his people,
　　shows mercy to his servants.

IV

¹⁵The idols of the nations are silver
　　and gold,
　　the work of human hands.
¹⁶They have mouths but do not
　　speak;
　　they have eyes but do not see;
¹⁷They have ears but do not hear;
　　nor is there breath in their
　　　mouths.
¹⁸Their makers will become like
　　them,
　　and anyone who trusts in them.

V

¹⁹House of Israel, bless the LORD!
　　House of Aaron, bless the LORD!
²⁰House of Levi, bless the LORD!

God granted the people as they moved through the wilderness and attempted to enter Canaan, the land of promise. The people would not have been able to accomplish such feats by their own power. They knew that it was God who, out of great concern ("mercy") for them, delivered and guided them. For that reason, God will be praised from generation to generation.

15-18 Worthlessness of other gods

Having extolled the marvels accomplished by the God of Israel, the psalmist proceeds to ridicule the gods of other nations. Though fashioned out of precious metals, they are simply the products of human making. They are not only devoid of divine powers, they cannot even do what human beings are able to perform. Finally, not only are they worthless, those who trust in them will be worthless like them.

19-21 A final call to praise

All are called on to bless or praise God. The house of Israel includes all the people. Explicit mention is made of those who serve in the sanctuary (cf. v. 2): the house of Aaron refers to the priests; the house of Levi refers to

You who fear the LORD, bless the
    LORD!
²¹Blessed be the LORD from Zion,
    who dwells in Jerusalem!
Hallelujah!

Hymn of Thanksgiving for God's Everlasting Mercy

136

I

¹Praise the LORD, for he is good;
    for his mercy endures forever;
²Praise the God of gods;
    for his mercy endures forever;
³Praise the Lord of lords;
    for his mercy endures forever;

II

⁴Who alone has done great
    wonders,
    for his mercy endures forever;
⁵Who skillfully made the heavens,
    for his mercy endures forever;
⁶Who spread the earth upon the
    waters,
    for his mercy endures forever;
⁷Who made the great lights,
    for his mercy endures forever;
⁸The sun to rule the day,
    for his mercy endures forever;
⁹The moon and stars to rule the
    night,
    for his mercy endures forever;

---

the Levites. Since fear of the Lord is the fundamental religious disposition of awe and reverence before God, those who possess this disposition would be the genuinely religious ones among the people. All Israel has been called on to praise the Lord who dwells in Jerusalem. The psalms ends as it began, with "Hallelujah!"

Psalm 136 (liturgical hymn)

1-3 A call to praise God

The liturgical character of this psalm is quite clear. Each verse ends with the refrain: "for his mercy endures forever." While each invocation was probably spoken by a liturgical leader, the refrain is meant for the entire congregation. This refrain is a statement of assurance that God's covenant love is eternal. Each of the first three verses is a summons to praise God. Three divine titles are employed. The LORD (YHWH) is the personal name of the God of Israel. This verse also provides a reason for the praise, namely, that God is good. The other two titles indicate that this God is superior to all other gods and to all other ruling lords.

4-9 Praise of the creator

God's exclusive divine power can be seen in the rule that God exercises over all the wonders of the heavens. It is this God who created the heavens and assigned the celestial bodies their stations, there to give off their light at the appropriate time; it is this God who harnessed the waters of the deep and spread out the earth on them. Such a God certainly deserves the praise of all.

III

10Who struck down the firstborn of Egypt,
  for his mercy endures forever;
11And led Israel from their midst,
  for his mercy endures forever;
12With mighty hand and out-stretched arm,
  for his mercy endures forever;
13Who split in two the Red Sea,
  for his mercy endures forever;
14And led Israel through its midst,
  for his mercy endures forever;
15But swept Pharaoh and his army into the Red Sea,
  for his mercy endures forever;

16Who led the people through the desert,
  for his mercy endures forever;

IV

17Who struck down great kings,
  for his mercy endures forever;
18Slew powerful kings,
  for his mercy endures forever;
19Sihon, king of the Amorites,
  for his mercy endures forever;
20Og, king of Bashan,
  for his mercy endures forever;
21And made their lands a heritage,
  for his mercy endures forever;
22A heritage for Israel, his servant,
  for his mercy endures forever.

10-16 God's exploits during the exodus

This mighty God is not only the creator of and ruler in the heavens and on the earth but also the one who delivered the Israelites from their cruel bondage in Egypt, a deliverance that was accomplished through miraculous signs and wonders. "[M]ighty hand and outstretched arm" symbolize the wondrous feats that God performed on Israel's behalf. Chief among these is the conquest of the sea. Though the reference here is to the geographic Reed Sea, behind the reference are allusions to the primordial chaotic waters over which God was triumphant at creation. Many ancient myths of origin recount how those waters were split and order was eventually established. In Israel's history, it was the evil of the pharaoh that was conquered, while the people of God were led to safety. The desert was a place of both testing and community consolidation. It was there that the motley group of survivors became a nation.

17-22 The land is occupied

In only a few short verses, Israel's struggle for the occupation of the land is recounted. It is important to note that Israel claims it was God, not simply the people's military prowess, that fended off those who would have prevented the occupation. In like manner, it was God who chose this land for the people in the first place. Israel would always regard this land as their heritage or inheritance, first promised and ultimately bestowed on them by a loving God.

V

²³The Lord remembered us in our
    low estate,
    for his mercy endures forever;
²⁴Freed us from our foes,
    for his mercy endures forever;
²⁵And gives bread to all flesh,
    for his mercy endures forever.

VI

²⁶Praise the God of heaven,
    for his mercy endures forever.

Sorrow and Hope in Exile

137

I

¹By the rivers of Babylon

there we sat weeping
    when we remembered Zion.
²On the poplars in its midst
    we hung up our harps.
³For there our captors asked us
    for the words of a song;
Our tormentors, for joy:
    "Sing for us a song of Zion!"
⁴But how could we sing a song of
    the LORD
    in a foreign land?

II

⁵If I forget you, Jerusalem,
    may my right hand forget.
⁶May my tongue stick to my palate
    if I do not remember you,

23-26 God's continued providence

The goodness of God is not limited to past favors. The wonders of creation and the deliverance from servitude may have transpired in the past, but God continues to shower blessings on this favored people. Therefore, it is fitting to continue to praise God.

Psalm 137 (communal lament)

1-4 The captives mourn

The psalm begins with a description of the sorrowful situation of the captives. The suffering of the people is not the result of physical assault at the hands of their enemies or of social oppression because of unjust laws and customs. Rather, it is soul-wrenching sorrow over the loss of their beloved city Jerusalem. In contrast, the triumphant city of Babylon has rivers that provide water to thriving poplar trees. Those who have captured the people ask them to sing a song of Zion. If the reference is to Israelite folk music, the request is for entertainment, which, under the circumstances, would be considered quite demeaning. If it is to religious music, the request would be blasphemous, for the Israelites could not envision praising God on foreign soil. In either case, such a request would have been seen as a form of mockery.

5-6 Self-curse

The psalmist calls down a self-curse to take effect if Jerusalem is ever forgotten. The consequences for infidelity are dire. A withered right hand

If I do not exalt Jerusalem
    beyond all my delights.

III

⁷Remember, LORD, against Edom
    that day at Jerusalem.
They said: "Level it, level it
    down to its foundations!"
⁸Desolate Daughter Babylon, you
    shall be destroyed,
    blessed the one who pays you
    back
    what you have done us!
⁹Blessed the one who seizes your
    children
    and smashes them against the
    rock.

Hymn of a Grateful Heart

138 ¹Of David.

I

I thank you, Lord, with all my
    heart;
    in the presence of the angels to
    you I sing.
²I bow low toward your holy
    temple;
    I praise your name for your
    mercy and faithfulness.
For you have exalted over all
    your name and your promise.
³On the day I cried out, you
    answered;
    you strengthened my spirit.

---

would make one incapable of work and, therefore, would relegate one to the margins of society. A paralyzed tongue would prevent one from speaking and would prevent one from participating fully in community life. According to Israel's strict laws of purity, one with any such disability would be considered a sinner who was so afflicted as punishment for some sin.

7-9 A curse on enemies

The last verses of this beautiful psalm are considered quite troublesome by many people today. Israel is actually calling down curses on those nations that have in any way acted against it. Edom, one of its neighbors to the east, not only refused Israel access through its territory when the people were originally entering the land of promise, but also participated in the looting of Jerusalem and the murder of its inhabitants at the time of its destruction by the Babylonians (cf. Obad 11-14). The most violent and disturbing image is of the children of Babylon being smashed against the rock. Without exonerating the violence, it is important to understand that, since children are the future of a people, Israel prayed for safety from any future conflict with Babylon. This scene also reveals the far-reaching horrors of any war.

Psalm 138 (prayer of confidence of an individual)

1-3 The prayer of thanksgiving

The psalmist is filled with gratitude because God responded to a desperate call for help. Homage is given to God and thanksgiving is offered

II

⁴All the kings of earth will praise
you, Lord,
when they hear the words of
your mouth.
⁵They will sing of the ways of the
Lord:
"How great is the glory of the
Lord!"
⁶The Lord is on high, but cares for
the lowly
and knows the proud from afar.
⁷Though I walk in the midst of
dangers,
you guard my life when my
enemies rage.
You stretch out your hand;
your right hand saves me.
⁸The Lord is with me to the end.

Lord, your mercy endures
forever.
Never forsake the work of your
hands!

The All-knowing and Ever-present God

139 ¹For the leader. A psalm of David.

I

Lord, you have probed me, you
know me:
²you know when I sit and stand;
you understand my thoughts
from afar.
³You sift through my travels and
my rest;

---

in the temple. The gods or heavenly beings were probably minor deities in the Canaanite pantheon, which, in Israel's religious scheme, remained a subservient part of God's council in heaven (cf. Ps 8:6; Job 1:6). Divine fidelity and steadfast love are characteristics of the covenant.

4-6 The exalted nature of God

Earlier, the psalmist sang of the greatness of the Lord. Now the rulers of other nations praise God. They too will exalt the goodness of God. The situation of the psalmist, once in need and then strengthened by God (cf. v. 3), is an example of how God cares for those who seek divine aid. Though God rules from the heavens, God is well aware of what transpires on earth and is attentive to the needs of the lowly.

7-8 Confidence in God

The psalmist knows from personal experience that God is ever-ready to help those in dire straits. God's right hand is the hand that wields salvific power. The psalmist declares that God's covenant love will last forever. This is the ground of all genuine confidence.

Psalm 139 (wisdom psalm)

1-6 God is all-knowing

This psalm is more a testimony to divine majesty than it is a prayer, though it does extol various divine characteristics. The psalmist maintains

with all my ways you are
    familiar.
⁴Even before a word is on my tongue,
    LORD, you know it all.
⁵Behind and before you encircle me
    and rest your hand upon me.
⁶Such knowledge is too wonderful
        for me,
    far too lofty for me to reach.
⁷Where can I go from your spirit?
    From your presence, where can I
        flee?
⁸If I ascend to the heavens, you are
        there;
    if I lie down in Sheol, there you
        are.

⁹If I take the wings of dawn
    and dwell beyond the sea,
¹⁰Even there your hand guides me,
    your right hand holds me fast.
¹¹If I say, "Surely darkness shall
        hide me,
    and night shall be my light"—
¹²Darkness is not dark for you,
    and night shines as the day.
    Darkness and light are but one.

II
¹³You formed my inmost being;
    you knit me in my mother's
        womb.

---

that God knows everything that happens and has insight into the innermost depths of an individual. In fact, God has such a grasp of one's thoughts that even the future is within the scope of divine comprehension. There is no place that is not under the all-knowing eye of God. Actually, God's comprehension is so thorough that it encircles the psalmist. This can be both reassuring and frightening. It all depends on the individual's disposition.

7-12 God is all-present

Besides being all-knowing, God is also omnipresent. The psalmist attempts to sketch the extent of the domain within which God reigns, a domain that reaches to the farthest limits of the heights and depths, as well as the expanse, of the earth. Early Israelite tradition did not include a well-defined notion of life after this life. While Israel did believe in a place inhabited by the dead, it was not clear that God exercised jurisdiction over it. The reference here seems to contradict that belief. The psalmist claims that God is indeed in Sheol. God rules over the highest heavens as well as the depths of Sheol. God is also present from the borders of the east, where dawn begins its flight across the horizon, to those of the west, the land on the other side of the sea. In other words, God is ever-present, guiding and caring for the psalmist. Finally, one might hope to look to darkness for concealment. Not so. Only creatures are hampered by the dark; light and darkness are the same to God. It is not that the psalmist is really trying to escape God. Rather, this is a poetic way of describing God's all-pervasive presence.

¹⁴I praise you, because I am
wonderfully made;
wonderful are your works!
My very self you know.
¹⁵My bones are not hidden from
you,
When I was being made in secret,
fashioned in the depths of the
earth.
¹⁶Your eyes saw me unformed;
in your book all are written
down;
my days were shaped, before
one came to be.

III

¹⁷How precious to me are your designs, O God;
how vast the sum of them!
¹⁸Were I to count them, they would
outnumber the sands;

when I complete them, still you
are with me.
¹⁹When you would destroy the
wicked, O God,
the bloodthirsty depart from
me!
²⁰Your foes who conspire a plot
against you
are exalted in vain.

IV

²¹Do I not hate, LORD, those who
hate you?
Those who rise against you, do I
not loathe?
²²With fierce hatred I hate them,
enemies I count as my own.
²³Probe me, God, know my heart;
try me, know my thoughts.
²⁴See if there is a wicked path in me;
lead me along an ancient path.

13-18 God creates with care

The inmost being is literally the kidneys, the seat of emotion and con-science. God possesses intimate knowledge of the psalmist, because God is the creator. The psalmist is in awe of the delicate care with which God fashions the human body within the mother's womb, like a weaver blend-ing skeins of material into an artistic creation (cf. Job 10:11). Although this marvelous fashioning takes place within the womb, hidden from sight like the mysteries of the earth's formation within the bowels of the earth, God is aware of every detail of human gestation. God's omniscience even in-cludes divine foreknowledge. This detailed description demonstrates the psalmist's appreciation of God's comprehensive knowledge, the scope of which the psalmist cannot even begin to fathom.

19-24 A plea for retribution

The psalm concludes on a somewhat negative note with the psalmist appealing to the theory of retribution: may the wicked be punished for their sinfulness. It is important to note that the psalmist does not assume the role of arbiter of right and wrong. That is God's right, and it is for God to exe-cute justice. These wicked have not only oppressed the psalmist, but have also blasphemed God's holy name. They are thus enemies of both, and so they are certainly deserving of punishment. Presumably, the psalmist has

Prayer for Deliverance from the Wicked

140 ¹For the leader. A psalm of David.

I

²Deliver me, LORD, from the
    wicked;
  preserve me from the violent,
³From those who plan evil in their
    hearts,
  who stir up conflicts every day,
⁴Who sharpen their tongue like a
    serpent,
  venom of asps upon their lips.

                              Selah

II

⁵Keep me, LORD, from the clutches
    of the wicked;
  preserve me from the violent,
  who plot to trip me up.
⁶The arrogant have set a trap for me;
  they have spread out ropes for a
    net,
  laid snares for me by the
    wayside.

                              Selah

⁷I say to the LORD: You are my God;
  listen, LORD, to the words of my
    pleas.
⁸LORD, my master, my strong
    deliverer,
  you cover my head on the day
    of armed conflict.

---

been faithful. Since God sees into the inmost recesses of the human heart, God would know this.

Psalm 140 (lament of an individual)

2-6 The cry of lament

The psalmist turns to God with two distinct yet very similar cries of lament. This double plea is for deliverance from the wicked, that is, those who set out to ruin the vulnerable psalmist with venomous lies and other traps. The violence from which the psalmist prays to be delivered is not physical assault. Rather, the Hebrew word employed means extreme wickedness. The psalmist is assailed by evil and seeks refuge from it in God.

7-8 A confession of faith

The titles with which the psalmist addresses God mark the manner in which the psalmist hopes God will act. The psalmist first declares, "You are my God." This statement claims that there is a relationship because of which the psalmist can presume divine assistance. The military title characterizes God as the bulwark of defense in time of battle. This is precisely the kind of help the psalmist needs at this time of crisis.

9-12 Punishment of the wicked

It is quite common for laments to include prayers that the wicked be punished for their sinfulness. The psalmist prays that the plans of the ene-

⁹Lord, do not grant the desires of
the wicked one;
do not let his plot succeed.

Selah

III

¹⁰Those who surround me raise
their heads;
may the mischief they threaten
overwhelm them.
¹¹Drop burning coals upon them;
cast them into the watery pit
never more to rise.
¹²Slanderers will not survive on
earth;
evil will hunt down the man of
violence to overthrow
him.

¹³For I know the Lord will take up
the cause of the needy,
justice for the poor.
¹⁴Then the righteous will give
thanks to your name;
the upright will dwell in your
presence.

Prayer for Deliverance from the Wicked

141 ¹A psalm of David.

Lord, I call to you; hasten to me;
listen to my plea when I call.
²Let my prayer be incense before
you;
my uplifted hands an evening
offering.

mies be thwarted and the wickedness that they plotted against the psalmist be turned against them instead. Some commentators maintain that the punishment for which the psalmist prays is more vengeance than it is justice. This is particularly true with regard to the fiery end that is envisioned. However, one cannot underestimate the threat posed to the delicate fabric of society by the kind of deceit and exploitation described here. If the society is to survive, such threats must be addressed.

13-14 Expressions of confidence

The lament ends on a note of confidence. The psalmist is certain that the evil will fall on those who perpetrated it. The just will be rescued and will give appropriate thanks to God.

Psalm 141 (lament of an individual)

1-2 A cry for help

The cry for help with which the psalm opens is short and to the point: "hasten." However, its brevity does not make it curt. On the contrary, the psalmist sees it as sweet-smelling as incense rising to God, and the traditional prayer stance of upraised arms is likened to an evening sacrifice offered in the temple.

³Set a guard, LORD, before my
mouth,
keep watch over the door of my
lips.
⁴Do not let my heart incline to evil,
to perform deeds in wickedness.
On the delicacies of evildoers
let me not feast.
⁵Let a righteous person strike me; it
is mercy if he reproves me.
Do not withhold oil from my
head
while my prayer opposes their
evil deeds.
⁶May their leaders be cast over the
cliff,
so that they hear that my
speeches are pleasing.
⁷Like the plowing and breaking up
of the earth,
our bones are strewn at the
mouth of Sheol.
⁸For my eyes are upon you, O
LORD, my Lord;
in you I take refuge; do not take
away my soul.
⁹Guard me from the trap they have
set for me,
from the snares of evildoers.
¹⁰Let the wicked fall into their own
nets,
while only I pass over them
safely.

3-4 The need for divine assistance

The possibility of being tempted to sin is always present. Therefore, the psalmist asks to be strengthened so as not to fail. While sins of speech are explicitly mentioned, there is an acknowledgment that evil really originates in the heart.

5-7 The right choice of company

The Hebrew of these verses is obscure. However, while the thoughts do not always seem to follow logically, it is clear that the psalmist is contrasting the company of the just with that of the wicked. The psalmist is also willing to be disciplined by the just. Just chastisement is compared to the steadfast love ("mercy") associated with the covenant. It might be considered a blessing, since it is meant to strengthen the psalmist's resolve to be faithful. Those cast over the cliff are probably the wicked. When this happens, the prayers of the righteous psalmist will be recognized by all as having been pleasing to God. An agricultural metaphor is employed to describe the fate of the wicked. They will be plowed, broken, and scattered at the entrance of Sheol.

8-10 A prayer for help

The psalm ends as it began, with a prayer to God for assistance when in need and protection from the schemes of evil perpetrators. The final words are for reversals of fortune: May they be caught in their own traps while I escape.

A Prayer in Time of Trouble

142 ¹A *maskil* of David, when he was in the cave. A prayer.

²With my own voice I cry to the
  LORD;
  with my own voice I beseech the
    LORD.
³Before him I pour out my
    complaint,
  tell of my distress in front of
    him.
⁴When my spirit is faint within me,
  you know my path.
As I go along this path,
  they have hidden a trap for me.
⁵I look to my right hand to see
  that there is no one willing to
    acknowledge me.

My escape has perished;
  no one cares for me.
⁶I cry out to you, LORD,
  I say, You are my refuge,
  my portion in the land of the
    living.
⁷Listen to my cry for help,
  for I am brought very low.
Rescue me from my pursuers,
  for they are too strong for me.
⁸Lead my soul from prison,
  that I may give thanks to your
    name.
Then the righteous shall gather
    around me
  because you have been good to
    me.

Psalm 142 (lament of an individual)

2-3 A cry of complaint

The cry of the psalmist is not muted. Rather, it is full-voiced and determined. The psalmist is intent on making God aware of the distress that has become such a terrible burden.

4-5 The path of suffering

The psalmist is vulnerable to the hidden traps set by attackers. There is no one along the way to help. God, who is aware of the course of events, is the psalmist's only hope, and so the afflicted one cries out to God for help.

6-8 The prayer for help

God is described as the psalmist's refuge, the only source of security. The land of the living signifies promise and full life. With God as surety, the psalmist is guaranteed life there and the peace and prosperity that come with divine blessing. Without God's help there is no hope, for the enemies are too strong for this sufferer. However, if God would step in and rescue the psalmist, this act of divine graciousness would be known to all, and all righteous people would marvel at God's goodness.

A Prayer in Distress

143 ¹A psalm of David.

LORD, hear my prayer;
in your faithfulness listen to my
pleading;
answer me in your righteousness.
²Do not enter into judgment with
your servant;
before you no one can be just.
³The enemy has pursued my soul;
he has crushed my life to the
ground.
He has made me dwell in darkness
like those long dead.
⁴My spirit is faint within me;
my heart despairs.
⁵I remember the days of old;
I ponder all your deeds;
the works of your hands I recall.
⁶I stretch out my hands toward you,
my soul to you like a parched
land.

Selah

Psalm 143 (lament of an individual; penitential)

1-2 A cry for help

Appeal is made to divine faithfulness and righteousness, two characteristics of God's covenant relationship with the psalmist. This relationship is underscored by the psalmist's own self-identification as servant of God. This servant is well aware of the impossibility of a person being just before God. Therefore, the prayer is also one of humble acknowledgment of human limitation.

3-4 The enemy attack

In this last of the penitential psalms (cf. Pss 6, 32, 38, 51, 102, 130) the psalmist's suffering is described. Enemies have had the upper hand. They have hounded the psalmist and smashed this defeated one to the ground. More than that, they have relegated the psalmist to a state of darkness that is as grim as death. All of this distress has taken its toll on the distraught one's inner being as well. The psalmist's state is pitiful. Surely God will respond.

5-6 Remembering past favors

Recalling past blessings can serve two related pressing religious concerns. As a reminder of God's beneficence in the past, it can instill hope in those who suffer, assured that God will act in a similarly gracious manner in the present. It can also spur the sufferer on to turn to God with this confidence and plead for relief. The image of a parched desert strikingly describes the psalmist's condition of longing for God.

[7]Hasten to answer me, LORD;
  for my spirit fails me.
Do not hide your face from me,
  lest I become like those descend-
        ing to the pit.
[8]In the morning let me hear of your
        mercy,
  for in you I trust.
Show me the path I should walk,
  for I entrust my life to you.
[9]Rescue me, LORD, from my foes,
  for I seek refuge in you.
[10]Teach me to do your will,
  for you are my God.
May your kind spirit guide me
  on ground that is level.
[11]For your name's sake, LORD, give
        me life;

in your righteousness lead my
        soul out of distress.
[12]In your mercy put an end to my
        foes;
  all those who are oppressing my
        soul,
  for I am your servant.

A Prayer for Victory and Prosperity

144 [1]Of David.

I

Blessed be the LORD, my rock,
  who trains my hands for battle,
  my fingers for war;
[2]My safeguard and my fortress,
  my stronghold, my deliverer,

7-12 Prayers for assistance

The lament ends as it began, with prayers for God's help. The psalmist cries to be heard. The pit is a reference to Sheol, the fate of the psalmist if God chooses not to respond. The possibility of experiencing divine mercy (covenant love) at dawn suggests a night vigil of prayer. The psalmist asks for both rescue from distress and direction for living. Though the latter implies a recommitment to a way of life in concert with covenant fidelity, there is no indication that the affliction that burdens the psalmist is punishment for some transgression. Rather, the psalmist has been faithful. It is the enemies who are guilty of transgression in their assault against this servant of God. The psalmist relies on God's kindness (covenant love) to set things right.

Psalm 144 (royal psalm)

1-2 Victory for the king

It is not until verse 10, with the mention of God's rescue of David, that the royal character of this psalm becomes apparent. The praise of God for having delivered the psalmist, with which this psalm opens, could have come from the mouth of any loyal Israelite. However, in this Davidic context, everything within the psalm takes on a decidedly royal character. Using military imagery, the psalmist ascribes all the king's military success to the power of God. God has been rock, fortress, stronghold, deliverer,

My shield, in whom I take refuge,
    who subdues peoples under me.

II

³LORD, what is man that you take
    notice of him;
    the son of man, that you think of
    him?
⁴Man is but a breath,
    his days are like a passing
    shadow.
⁵LORD, incline your heavens and
    come down;
    touch the mountains and make
    them smoke.
⁶Flash forth lightning and scatter
    my foes;
    shoot your arrows and rout
    them.
⁷Reach out your hand from on high;

deliver me from the many waters;
    rescue me from the hands of
    foreign foes.
⁸Their mouths speak untruth;
    their right hands are raised in
    lying oaths.
⁹O God, a new song I will sing to
    you;
    on a ten-stringed lyre I will play
    for you.
¹⁰You give victory to kings;
    you delivered David your
    servant.
From the menacing sword ¹¹deliver
    me;
    rescue me from the hands of
    foreign foes.
Their mouths speak untruth;
    their right hands are raised in
    lying oaths.

---

shield, and defender. The king has simply been the beneficiary of divine goodness.

3-4 Human frailty

The psalmist marvels at God's concern for human beings (cf. Ps 8:5). Human strength, which is nothing compared with divine power, is as fragile as a breath of air, as fleeting as a momentary shadow. Despite such obvious frailty, God cares for humankind.

5-8 A prayer for help

This is a request for a manifestation of divine power. God was frequently revealed amid extraordinary occurrences in nature. Mountains quaked; the heavens thundered; lightning split the sky (cf. Exod 19:16). Here God is asked to rescue the psalmist in just such an awe-inspiring manner. This kind of phenomenal appearance of divine power would silence the psalmist's enemies and leave them quaking in the presence of such majesty.

9-11 A promise to praise God

The victory that God has already bestowed on various kings and on David in particular is employed as incentive for the deliverance of the psalmist from the lying speech of the enemies. This latter favor is then the occasion of singing a new song of praise to God.

III

12May our sons be like plants
    well nurtured from their youth,
Our daughters, like carved columns,
    shapely as those of the temple.
13May our barns be full
    with every kind of store.
May our sheep increase by
    thousands,
    by tens of thousands in our
      fields;
    may our oxen be well fattened.
14May there be no breach in the
    walls,
    no exile, no outcry in our streets.
15Blessed the people so fortunate;
    blessed the people whose God is
    the LORD.

The Greatness and Goodness of God

145 1Praise. Of David.

I will extol you, my God and king;
    I will bless your name forever
      and ever.
2Every day I will bless you;
    I will praise your name forever
      and ever.
3Great is the LORD and worthy of
    much praise,
    whose grandeur is beyond
      understanding.
4One generation praises your deeds
    to the next
    and proclaims your mighty
      works.

12-15 A benediction

The section ends with a beatitude, a typical wisdom form that demonstrates the happiness that one finds by following the way mapped out by God. The entire section, however, contains several statements that are similar to beatitudes: May your sons be filled with life's potency so that the family bloodline will endure; may your daughters be beautifully fashioned so that they will honor the family; may your flocks increase and your fields produce abundantly; may your cities resist any attack from the outside. The actual beatitude (v. 15) gathers all of these people together and identifies them as blessed. They are particularly blessed because they are the Lord's own people.

Psalm 145 (hymn)

1-3 Praise of God

In traditional hymnic fashion, the psalm opens with an acclamation of praise. God is exalted as the divine king whose greatness cannot be fathomed. Words cannot even begin to describe God's wondrous nature, and so the psalmist resorts to repetitious exclamation and superlatives. In the midst of this exuberant praise, the psalmist promises to sing God's glories everywhere and forever.

4-9 Continuous praise

The psalmist is not alone in praising God. Generation after generation recalls the wondrous deeds performed by God, and each generation joins

⁵They speak of the splendor of your
majestic glory,
tell of your wonderful deeds.
⁶They speak of the power of your
awesome acts
and recount your great deeds.
⁷They celebrate your abounding
goodness
and joyfully sing of your justice.
⁸The Lord is gracious and merciful,
slow to anger and abounding in
mercy.
⁹The Lord is good to all,
compassionate toward all your
works.
¹⁰All your works give you thanks,
Lord
and your faithful bless you.

¹¹They speak of the glory of your
reign
and tell of your mighty works,
¹²Making known to the sons of men
your mighty acts,
the majestic glory of your rule.
¹³Your reign is a reign for all ages,
your dominion for all
generations.
The Lord is trustworthy in all his
words,
and loving in all his works.
¹⁴The Lord supports all who are
falling
and raises up all who are bowed
down.
¹⁵The eyes of all look hopefully to
you;

the next in singing God's praises. God's "mighty works" is usually a reference to the wonders God accomplished in delivering Israel from the bondage of Egypt. In this regard, God's justice was seen in the release of this chosen people from oppression. This interpretation of the reference is reinforced by the description of God: "The Lord is gracious and merciful, / slow to anger and abounding in mercy." The phrase first appears in the account of the renewal of the covenant in the wilderness after the people had sinned by worshiping the golden calf (cf. Exod 34:6). The phrase not only contains covenant vocabulary (mercy and love), but is a reminder that this promise was made with people who had only recently violated their covenant commitment. Divine mercy and love take on a distinctive character in such circumstances. It is precisely this mercy toward sinners, and not merely divine splendor generally, that is being praised in this psalm.

10-14 Divine rule

The universal rule of God is extolled. This rule is characterized by its glory, its power, and its eternal duration. God has no rival; all creatures, generation after generation, are under this divine dominion, and all creatures praise God for the glorious nature of this rule. God seems particularly attentive to the needs of the weak and afflicted, lifting them up when they fall. Such kindness is in keeping with a nature that is merciful and compassionate.

15-21 God cares for the needy

God's prodigal generosity to the needy is proclaimed. God cares for them with open hands, refusing nothing. Covenant love ("merciful," v. 17)

you give them their food in due
season.
[16]You open wide your hand
and satisfy the desire of every
living thing.
[17]The LORD is just in all his ways,
merciful in all his works.
[18]The LORD is near to all who call
upon him,
to all who call upon him in
truth.
[19]He fulfills the desire of those who
fear him;
he hears their cry and saves
them.
[20]The LORD watches over all who
love him,
but all the wicked he destroys.

[21]My mouth will speak the praises
of the LORD;
all flesh will bless his holy name
forever and ever.

Trust in God the Creator and Redeemer

146 [1]Hallelujah!

[2]Praise the LORD, my soul;
I will praise the LORD all my life,
sing praise to my God while I
live.

I

[3]Put no trust in princes,
in children of Adam powerless
to save.

---

is extolled, as is another covenant characteristic, faithfulness ("truth," v. 18). Fear of God is the disposition of awe and reverence. Those who possess this disposition turn to God and rely on divine assistance. They will not be disappointed. God will hear their cry and come to their aid. This is reason for praising God.

HALLELUJAH PSALMS (146–50)

The last five psalms of this book and of the entire Psalter are known as the "Hallelujah Psalms," because they begin and end with that traditional acclamation. None of these psalms has a superscription, and all of them are hymns.

Psalm 146 (hymn)

1-2 Praise of God

The psalm opens with the standard call to praise God: "Hallelujah!" This is followed by a second call to praise and a promise that the psalmist will do so throughout all of life.

3-4 Human rule is not to be trusted

The psalmist warns against putting trust in human rule which is dependent on the person in power. Human beings are mortal and human rule collapses with the death of the ruler. Any security that may have existed in

◄ ⁴Who breathing his last, returns to
the earth;
  that day all his planning comes
  to nothing.

II

⁵Blessed the one whose help is the
God of Jacob,
  whose hope is in the LORD, his
  God,
⁶The maker of heaven and earth,
  the seas and all that is in them,
Who keeps faith forever,
  ⁷secures justice for the oppressed,
  who gives bread to the hungry.
The LORD sets prisoners free;

⁸the LORD gives sight to the
blind.
The LORD raises up those who are
  bowed down;
  the LORD loves the righteous.
⁹The LORD protects the resident
alien,
  comes to the aid of the orphan
  and the widow,
  but thwarts the way of the
  wicked.
¹⁰The LORD shall reign forever,
  your God, Zion, through all
  generations!
Hallelujah!

---

society is then lost, and the people are often thrown into confusion with no direction. It is foolish to trust in something so fragile and transitory.

5-9 The trustworthiness of God

In contrast to the futility of trust in human beings, the psalmist testifies to the wisdom of trusting in God. This wisdom is stated by means of a beatitude. Those who turn to God for help will find that God is more than trustworthy. God has the power and authority to accomplish whatever one requests, for God is the creator of heaven and earth. God is the one who formed the sea, once thought to be the primordial monster of chaos. God also exercises power and authority on earth. What follows may be reminiscent of some of the favors Israel experienced from the hand of God when the people were in dire straits. One item in the list also reflects an aspect of the social obligations on which Israelite society was based. This was care for the stranger, the orphan, and the widow, three classes of people who lacked male legal protection within the patriarchal society. Their mention here shows that the God of Israel is attentive to the needs of the most vulnerable in the community.

10 Praise of God

The final verse contains an acclamation of divine sovereignty. It is precisely the God of Israel who will reign forever. It is this God in whom all should place their trust. The psalm ends as it began, with an exclamation of praise: "Hallelujah!"

God's Word Restores Jerusalem

147 ¹Hallelujah!

I

How good to sing praise to our
    God;
    how pleasant to give fitting
        praise.
²The LORD rebuilds Jerusalem,
    and gathers the dispersed of
        Israel,
³Healing the brokenhearted,
    and binding up their wounds.
⁴He numbers the stars,
    and gives to all of them their
        names.
⁵Great is our Lord, vast in power,
    with wisdom beyond measure.
⁶The LORD gives aid to the poor,
    but casts the wicked to the
        ground.

II

⁷Sing to the LORD with thanksgiving;
    with the lyre make music to our
        God,
⁸Who covers the heavens with
        clouds,
    provides rain for the earth,
    makes grass sprout on the
        mountains,
⁹Who gives animals their food
    and young ravens what they cry
        for.
¹⁰He takes no delight in the strength
    of horses,
    no pleasure in the runner's
        stride.
¹¹Rather the LORD takes pleasure in
    those who fear him,
    those who put their hope in his
        mercy.

Psalm 147 (hymn)

1-6 The graciousness of God

The first section of the psalm opens with a declaration to celebrate God's saving power in song. This is followed by a listing of some of the wondrous deeds that God performed for the people of Israel. These are the reasons for giving praise. Mention of the restoration of Jerusalem and of the return of the scattered people dates the psalm in the postexilic period. God's goodness to the poor and needy is acclaimed.

7-11 The power of God

The second section opens with a summons to thank God in song. The reasons for praise are the glories of creation. In ancient Canaanite mythology, the clouds were the chariot of the great storm deity. Here they are simply the covering for the heavens, both of which are creatures of God. This same God is the source of water and fertility, the one who provides food for all living beings. Despite all the marvels of the created world, God takes greatest delight in devout hearts.

III

¹²Glorify the LORD, Jerusalem;
   Zion, offer praise to your God,
¹³For he has strengthened the bars
      of your gates,
   blessed your children within
      you.
¹⁴He brings peace to your borders,
   and satisfies you with finest
      wheat.
¹⁵He sends his command to earth;
   his word runs swiftly!
¹⁶Thus he makes the snow like
      wool,
   and spreads the frost like ash;
¹⁷He disperses hail like crumbs.
   Who can withstand his cold?
¹⁸Yet when again he issues his com-
      mand, it melts them;
   he raises his winds and the
      waters flow.

¹⁹He proclaims his word to Jacob,
   his statutes and laws to Israel.
²⁰He has not done this for any other
      nation;
   of such laws they know nothing.
Hallelujah!

All Creation Summoned To Praise

148 ¹Hallelujah!

I

Praise the LORD from the heavens;
   praise him in the heights.
²Praise him, all you his angels;
   give praise, all you his hosts.
³Praise him, sun and moon;
   praise him, all shining stars.
⁴Praise him, highest heavens,
   you waters above the heavens.

12-20 The providence of God

For a third time, the people are called to praise God. Here the address is directed to the city of Jerusalem. There is no chronological order in the listing of favors granted by God. The city itself has been fortified, and peace reigns within it. Praise is given to the God who controls the powers of nature as well as the forces of history. All of this is done for the sake of the people of Israel. Mention of divine law is a reference to the covenant pact made with this chosen people. The psalm ends as it began, with the exclamation of praise: "Hallelujah!"

Psalm 148 (hymn)

1-6 Praise from the heavens

Besides the initial summons: "Hallelujah," the call to praise appears seven times in this section. All the celestial beings are invited to praise the Lord. The sun, moon, and stars, considered deities in other ancient cultures, are creatures of God called on to sing praise to the creator. The heights of the heavens is the place of greatest honor; the hosts are military units of angelic defenders; the waters above the heavens are part of the original chaotic flood that was quelled by God and then assigned its place above

⁵Let them all praise the LORD's
name;
for he commanded and they
were created,
⁶Assigned them their station forever,
set an order that will never
change.

II

⁷Praise the LORD from the earth,
you sea monsters and all the
deeps of the sea;
⁸Lightning and hail, snow and thick
clouds,
storm wind that fulfills his
command;
⁹Mountains and all hills,
fruit trees and all cedars;

¹⁰Animals wild and tame,
creatures that crawl and birds
that fly;
¹¹Kings of the earth and all peoples,
princes and all who govern on
earth;
¹²Young men and women too,
old and young alike.
¹³Let them all praise the LORD's
name,
for his name alone is exalted,
His majesty above earth and
heaven.
¹⁴He has lifted high the horn of his
people;
to the praise of all his faithful,
the Israelites, the people near to
him.
Hallelujah!

the firmament (cf. Gen 1:7). Every aspect of the heavenly realm was created by God and continues under God's control. They are all called on to sing praise to the Lord.

7-13 Praise from the earth

All the creatures of the earth are summoned to praise God. The sea monsters and the ocean depths have mythological connotations. Originally they were chaotic forces (cf. Isa 27:1; Gen 1:2). Storm elements were also considered minor deities, agents of the mighty storm god. Here, they are called on to praise the creator along with the wonders of the earth, the animals that live on it, and the fruits that it produces. Formerly the rulers of other nations paid homage to their respective gods. Now they too are invited to praise the God of Israel. Despite the class distinctions normally present in strict patriarchal societies, there is neither gender nor age exclusion. All are invited to praise the name of the Lord.

14 Israel is favored

The horn is a symbol of strength. This God who is to be praised by everything in the heavens and on the earth has singled Israel out for special honor. The psalm ends as it began: "Hallelujah!"

Praise God with Song and Sword

149 ¹Hallelujah!

Sing to the LORD a new song,
   his praise in the assembly of the
     faithful.
²Let Israel be glad in its maker,
   the people of Zion rejoice in
     their king.
³Let them praise his name in dance,
   make music with tambourine
     and lyre.
⁴For the LORD takes delight in his
     people,
   honors the poor with victory.
⁵Let the faithful rejoice in their
     glory,
   cry out for joy on their couches,
⁶With the praise of God in their
     mouths,

and a two-edged sword in their
     hands,
⁷To bring retribution on the nations,
   punishment on the peoples,
⁸To bind their kings in shackles,
   their nobles in chains of iron,
⁹To execute the judgments decreed
     for them—
   such is the glory of all God's
     faithful.
Hallelujah!

Final Doxology

150 ¹Hallelujah!

Praise God in his holy sanctuary;
   give praise in the mighty dome
     of heaven.
²Give praise for his mighty deeds,
   praise him for his great majesty.

Psalm 149 (hymn)

1-5 A communal celebration

The psalm opens with the standard summons to praise: "Hallelujah!" The setting is a liturgical assembly with music, festive dancing, and banqueting. The occasion is the celebration of the kingship of God. The psalmist calls for a new song, perhaps because of some victory that God granted the people in return for their fidelity.

6-9 A victory celebration

It is clear that this is a celebration of victory over enemies. The two-edged sword, which cuts both ways, executes both justice and the punishment due those who have acted as enemies of God's people and, therefore, as enemies of God. The psalm ends as it began: "Hallelujah!"

Psalm 150 (hymn)

1-6 A liturgical celebration

The entire psalm is a paean of praise. With the exception of the last verse, every line begins with a call to praise. The long list of musical instruments indicates that the occasion is a liturgical celebration. There is some question about the setting of this celebration. The sanctuary is certainly the temple

³Give praise with blasts upon the
    horn,
    praise him with harp and lyre.
⁴Give praise with tambourines and
    dance,
    praise him with strings and pipes.

⁵Give praise with crashing cymbals,
    praise him with sounding cym-
    bals.
⁶Let everything that has breath
    give praise to the LORD!
Hallelujah!

---

in Jerusalem, but the dome of heaven suggests God's celestial tabernacle. Every element in the psalm indicates that the celebration is on earth. It may be that the heavenly dome is mentioned for poetic reasons and because the earthly temple was considered a reflection of the heavenly sanctuary. The psalm ends as it began: "Hallelujah!" It is fitting that the entire Psalter ends in this way.

REVIEW AIDS AND DISCUSSION TOPICS

Introduction to the Book of Psalms *(pages 5–11)*

1. To whom is attributed authorship of the majority of psalms in the third book?

2. What characterizes the fifth book of psalms?

3. Why does the enumeration of verses vary among different translations of the Psalms?

4. How is the literary technique of parallelism used in the psalms?

5. To what might the word "Selah" refer?

6. What messages are conveyed by the different types of psalms?

7. If the original authors did not have Christ in mind when composing the psalms, is it wrong for Christians to see Christ in the psalms today?

8. What is a "covenant partner" and how does that characterize Israel's relationship to the Lord? What implications does that have for understanding who God is?

9. How do the psalms approach life after death? What implications does that have for reading how they depict life *before* death?

10. How can we appreciate what is offensive in the psalms (e.g., violence, male bias, cultural superiority complexes)?

11. What can we make of the warrior imagery in the psalms?

Book Three: Psalms 73–89 *(pages 13–50)*

1. Psalm 78. What is unique about this psalm and its purpose?

2. Psalm 79. To what historical event might this psalm be a response?

3. Psalm 80. What is the significance of the "vine" imagery used here? What other scriptural passages use this metaphor?

4. Psalm 84. What is the Baca valley? What might it represent?

5. Psalm 87. What may the psalmist mean by claims that Jerusalem is the birthplace (or "mother") of other cities and nations? (There is more than one answer here.)

6. Psalm 88. What is Sheol and why does the psalmist consider it unpleasant?

7. Psalm 89. How does the psalmist reinterpret the ancient concept that kings were descended from gods?

Book Four: Psalms 90–106 *(pages 51–82)*

1. Psalm 90. Compare the psalmist's descriptions of God's time and human time.

2. Psalm 92. What is the relationship between "folly" and "sin"?

3. Psalm 102. What metaphors are used to describe the psalmist's distress?

4. Psalm 104. How does the psalmist adapt other works of religious literature from the ancient Near East? What makes this psalm different?

5. Psalms 105–6. How do these two psalms differ in their recitation of history?

Book Five: Psalms 107–150 *(pages 82–149)*

1. Psalm 109. What are two ways in which commentators have interpreted this psalm? Do you find one more convincing than the other?

2. Psalm 110. Who is Melchizedek and what does this psalmist have to say about him? Where else does this figure appear in Scripture?

3. Psalm 118. This psalm of thanksgiving is often used in celebrations throughout the Easter season. What appears to be the original context of this psalm, and how does that lend itself to adaptation?

4. Psalm 119. How does this psalm characterize the law and a life of covenant faithfulness?

5. Psalm 127. What is the psalmist's attitude toward children?

6. Psalm 131. How does the psalmist use the image of a mother and child? What is being communicated here?

7. Psalm 137. Surely the psalmist would want to sing a song of Zion. Why is that not the case here?

8. Psalm 139. How is God characterized throughout this psalm?

9. Psalm 141. The psalmist's call for God's attention may strike some as brusque. How is this not the case?

10. Psalm 146. Why does the psalmist single out resident aliens, orphans, and widows?

INDEX OF CITATIONS FROM THE
CATECHISM OF THE CATHOLIC CHURCH

The arabic number(s) following the citation refer(s) to the paragraph number(s) in the *Catechism of the Catholic Church*.

79:9	431	104:27	2828	119:30	2465
82:6	441	104:30	292, 703	119:90	2465
84:3	1770	105:3	30	119:105	141
85:11	214	106:23	2577	119:142	2465
85:12	2795	107:20	1502	119:160	215
88:11-13	633	110	447	121:2	1605
89	709	110:1	659	124:8	287
89:49	633	110:4	1537	130:1	2559
91:10-13	336	111:9	2807	130:3	370
95:1-6	2628	113:1-2	2143	131:2	239
95:7-8	2659	115:3	268, 303	131:2-3	370
95:7	1165	115:4-5	2112	134:3	287
95:9	2119	115:8	2112	135:6	269
95:10	539	115:15	216, 287	138	304
96:2	2143	115:16	326, 326	138:2	214
102:27-28	212	116:12	224	139:15	2270
103	304	116:13	1330	143:10	1831
103:20	329	116:17	1330	145:3	300
104	288	118:14	1808	145:9	295, 342
104:13-15	1333	118:24	2173	146:3-4	150
104:15	1293	118:22	587, 756		
104:24	295	118:26	559		